The Impacts of Green Space on Student Experience at an Urban Community College

This book presents a rich case study examining physical and spatial factors of urban campus design that influence student experience and wellbeing.

The text details important historical context illustrating the foundational concepts and purpose of college sites in the United States and maps economic reforms and policies which have driven the development of today's inner-city campuses. Focusing on Bronx Community College, New York, and looking specifically at how the presence or absence of green space impacts students, the text then draws on diverse student voices to examine how students use open spaces, and how this influences their sense of belonging, stress reduction, and scholarly identities. The author's historical and qualitative research presents original insights and relies on a rich body of textual and on-site investigation.

This book will be a valuable resource for researchers and academics with an interest in urban education and higher education. It will be of particular interest to those with a focus on multicultural education and education policy.

Vanita Naidoo teaches sociology at the State University of New York (SUNY). She completed her PhD at The CUNY Graduate Center, USA.

Routledge Research in Higher Education

Higher Education, State Repression, and Neoliberal Reform in Nicaragua
Reflections from a University under Fire
Edited by Wendi Bellanger, Serena Cosgrove, and Irina Carlota Silber

The Past, Present, and Future of Higher Education in the Arabian Gulf Region
Critical Comparative Perspectives in a Neoliberal Era
Edited by Awad Ibrahim and Osman Z. Barnawi

Students' Experiences of Psychosocial Problems in Higher Education
Battling and Belonging
Edited by Trine Wulf-Andersen, Lene Larsen, Annie Aarup Jensen, Lone Krogh, Aske Basselbjerg Stigemo, Mathias Hulgård Kristiansen

Dismantling Constructs of Whiteness in Higher Education
Narratives of Resistance from the Academy
Edited by Teresa Y. Neely and Margie Montañez

The Impacts of Green Space on Student Experience at an Urban Community College
An Exploration of Wellbeing, Belonging, and Scholarly Identity
Vanita Naidoo

Enhancing Values of Dignity, Democracy, and Diversity in Higher Education
Comparative Insights for Challenging Times
Edited by Tamar Ketko, Hana Bor, and Khalid Arar

For more information about this series, please visit: www.routledge.com/Routledge-Research-in-Higher-Education/book-series/RRHE

The Impacts of Green Space on Student Experience at an Urban Community College

An Exploration of Wellbeing, Belonging, and Scholarly Identity

Vanita Naidoo

NEW YORK AND LONDON

First published 2023
by Routledge
605 Third Avenue, New York, NY 10158

and by Routledge
4 Park Square, Milton Park, Abingdon, Oxon, OX14 4RN

Routledge is an imprint of the Taylor & Francis Group, an informa business

© 2023 Vanita Naidoo

The right of Vanita Naidoo to be identified as author of this work has been asserted in accordance with sections 77 and 78 of the Copyright, Designs and Patents Act 1988.

All rights reserved. No part of this book may be reprinted or reproduced or utilised in any form or by any electronic, mechanical, or other means, now known or hereafter invented, including photocopying and recording, or in any information storage or retrieval system, without permission in writing from the publishers.

Trademark notice: Product or corporate names may be trademarks or registered trademarks, and are used only for identification and explanation without intent to infringe.

Library of Congress Cataloging-in-Publication Data
A catalog record for this title has been requested

ISBN: 9780367672768 (hbk)
ISBN: 9780367672805 (pbk)
ISBN: 9781003130598 (ebk)

DOI: 10.4324/9781003130598

Typeset in Times New Roman
by Apex CoVantage, LLC

To the students at Bronx Community College who made this study possible.

Contents

Foreword   x
Preface   xii
Acknowledgments   xiii
Glossary   xiv

1 Introduction: Early Historical Context for the American Higher Education System and US Campus Design   1

Defining the American Higher Education System 2
Brief History of Higher Education in America 2
The Birth of the Community College 4
The Impact of the Truman Commission 5
Defining the Community College 6
How the College Functions 8
Policy and Funding 9
Policies of Space 10
A Bronx Tale: The Community College 10
The Master Plan 11
Negotiation 12
The Campus 12

2 The Interaction Between Learning Space and Experience: Wellbeing, Belonging, and Scholarly Identity   15

Campus as Place 15
Early U.S. Campus Formations 16
Space for Intellectual Exchange 17

viii *Contents*

    Wellbeing 17
    Reactions and Perceptions 19
    Politics of Privacy 20
    Private Versus Public 22
    Belonging 24
    Belonging and Restorative Experience 25
    Mapping and Affordance of Space 26
    Scholarly Identity 27
    Characteristics of Space 28
    Symbolic Qualities of the Campus 28

3 A Study on Bronx Community College: Rationale and Methodology 31

    Research Questions 33
    Stage One (Survey) 33
    Survey Design and Campus Design 35
    Definitions of Natural Space 35
    Wellbeing in the Survey Design 36
    Belonging in the Survey Design 37
    Scholarly Identity in the Survey Design 37
    Stage Two (Focus Group) 38
    Campus Design in the Focus Group 39
    Wellbeing in the Focus Group 39
    Belonging in the Focus Group 40
    Scholarly Identity in the Focus Group 40
    A Brief History of CUNY 41
    New York and Higher Education 42
    Rationale for Study 42

4 Student Perception, Use, and Wellbeing on Campus 46

    Survey Analysis 46
    Profile of the Survey Participants 47
    Time Outside 48
    Comfort 49
    Social Interaction 51
    Wellbeing 51
    Scholarly Identity 52
    Campus Use 52

Focus Group Analysis 52
Scholarly Identity 53
Social Interactions 54
Belonging 57
Wellbeing 62

5 **Looking Forward: Outcomes and Implications for Future Campus Design and Development**   71

Time 72
The Oasis 74
Uses of Green Space 75
Future Areas of Analysis 76
On-Campus Housing 76
Faculty and Staff 77
Landmarks 77
Demographics 78
Community 78
Campus as Place 79
Green Spaces on Campus: Wellbeing, Belonging, and
   Scholarly Identity 80
Wellbeing 81
Belonging 82
Scholarly Identity 83
Looking Forward 83

Afterword	85
Appendix A: Survey Questions	91
Appendix B: Focus Group	97
Index	99

Foreword

For those of us who have taught and studied at the City University of New York (CUNY), we very deeply recognize how, often, the scarcity of space influences how we construct our lives around the notion of "college." In sharp contrast to Hollywood's version of the residential college campuses that span acres of vast, green lawns, surrounded by wrought-iron gates punctuated by picturesque quadrangles, college life in New York City mirrors that of city living. In Manhattan, we imagine the never-ending skyscrapers, or the hustle and bustle found on every corner that identify this iconic location. The Borough of Manhattan Community College occupies a suite of high-rise buildings in the shadow of the World Trade Center. But, for the tourist on foot, the campus looks much like the architecture of its environs and could easily be mistaken for just another in a series of office buildings. Further north in Midtown is Guttman Community College, the newest addition to CUNY. Occupying prime real estate in Manhattan, the seven-story building matches its corporate context as it overlooks the picturesque Bryant Park with Times Square to its west and the New York Public Library and Grand Central Terminal to the east. There are exceptions, though, once one leaves the central business district that has long been Manhattan's core identity.

Dr. Vanita Naidoo takes us to The Bronx, a borough often associated with Yankee Stadium or urban aesthetic that gently shifts to spacious freestanding homes before meeting the suburban landscape of Westchester County. In this compelling narrative grounded in rich history, Naidoo artfully explores the complexity of campus life in one of the largest cities in the world. Bronx Community College is nestled on a luscious green campus adjacent to the banks of the Harlem River in the University Heights neighborhood of one of New York's most complex and deeply influential boroughs. Bronx Community College has a vastly different campus than many CUNY colleges. It resembles a more traditional park campus with buildings separated from one another by rolling green space. It is, in many ways, separated from the torrent of traffic that cascades up and down the grand boulevards of The Bronx. As Naidoo brings forward from her focused study, students and staff alike see the campus as a respite, a place to socialize and to think, and a space for thoughtful reflection.

Dr. Naidoo very accurately describes the tensions and contradictions of city life and how one of New York's oldest community colleges helps people grow their social and professional networks in a place that can feel both overwhelming and incredibly isolating. Most of our work as higher education policy researchers focuses on the internal processes of the college itself and fails to understand how physical space influences and impacts one's relationship to learning. Dr. Naidoo does that here. She takes us to the campus itself in the time before COVID, to a moment in history where New York City thrived off an insatiable energy. She documents a time between two crises, a period between the Great Recession and the Great Pandemic. Enrollments were on the rise and a diverse cross section of American society was finding a pathway to the middle class through the community college. And, on campuses like Bronx Community College, students, faculty, and staff were bumping into one another on the quad, faces free of the cover of masks, to have a quick conversation before heading to class. It seems like a different time. And so, it was.

Vanita Naidoo tells us the story of what happens outside of the classroom in the informal spaces we create with one another over shared ideas and experiences. She takes us to one of the most interesting cultural places in the world and delivers a complex narrative of one of the nation's greatest community colleges. It is, indeed, a Bronx tale.

Chet Jordan, PhD
Interim Vice President of Academic Affairs
Greenfield Community College

Preface

> It is undeniable that in some parts of the Academy, located on the margins of Athens, was a self-enclosed *paradeisos* . . . detached from the tumult of city life (p. 67).
>
> —Robert Pogue Harrison, Gardens: An Essay in the Human Condition (2008)

This book reflects on the social and political dimensions of physical space. It also offers a discussion of policy and design choices that have shaped the American college campus. As a Canadian who has had the opportunity to work and study abroad, the American higher education system has left a lasting impression with its fierce contradictions and an ever-present desire for change. This study establishes a brief timeline on the origin of postsecondary education in the United States while the community college and the CUNY system inform the exploration of student experience.

On a personal note, I can't help but recall a story my mother told me about growing up in South Africa. She explained that when she was a girl her non-white public school inherited a building from an elite private institution that had relocated to another part of the city. I remember being struck by that idea because I never imagined a building could be given away and in turn belong to a new set of students. Looking back that story likely inspired my curiosity about the politics of space, which is inherently tied to potential, privilege, and place.

Through the rich commentary of students at Bronx Community College, this book continues the conversation my mother started all those years ago.

Reference

Harrison, R. P. (2008) *Gardens: An Essay on the Human Condition.* Chicago: University of Chicago Press.

Acknowledgments

First and foremost, my gratitude to the students at Bronx Community College (BCC). In addition, I would like to thank my colleague and classmate Dr. Meghan Moore-Wilk for access to the CUNY archives on Bronx Community College. My thanks to Dr. Alexander Ott, Dean at BCC's Department of Academic Success and President Isekenegbe, both of whom generously assisted me on campus. I am also deeply grateful to Donal Farley's wonderful memory and the invaluable detail he shared on the historic acquisition of NYU's campus in the Heights. This book is the product of my time at graduate school so I would like to acknowledge the unfailing guidance of my advisor Dr. Anthony Picciano. His career at CUNY, passion for higher education and Bronx origins shaped my experience as a doctoral student. Thanks for taking me on that journey, one always made richer by conversations with David Chapin about the benefits of supportive space and the steadfast encouragement of Dr. David Bloomfield. On a personal note, I appreciate the endless support, Dr. Chet Jordan, Interim Vice President of Academic Affairs at Greenfield Community College, has given me throughout the years. Thank you to my family for always being there and mostly to my partner, who makes everything possible.

Glossary

Academical Village—is a concept created by Thomas Jefferson that emphasized the idea of community and that fostered meaningful exchange between faculty and student. It was a location that was defined by an academic experience, unique to this environment.

Affordance—what an object offers a person, what it provides or furnishes. Positive and negative affordances are delineated in terms of what one may be able to do with an object versus how an object creates an obstacle or a barrier.

Attention Restoration Theory—the experience of fascination (effortless attention) allows directed attention to stop for recovery. Natural environments are rich in the characteristics necessary for restorative experiences that lead to recovery from fatigue.

Back Yard—a space, designated for faculty, staff, and students that is defined by its three-sided enclosure and is a private space used for more intimate encounters between smaller groups of people either talking or eating on campus. The effect of a cozy or quiet atmosphere is increased by being located behind a building.

Cottage System—an American construction of campus buildings that separates structures to form a patchwork of academic units that are "park like" in structure.

Directed Attention—involves effortful attention.

Fascination—involves effortless attention.

Front Porch—outdoor spaces that lead directly into frequented buildings such as departments or common areas. They have a physical and psychological quality that offers cues for the student to transition from one type of behavior to another.

Front Yard—spaces where students feel it is acceptable to relax, sunbathe, or mediate in a public space on campus because it is familiar, and they are surrounded by people they know or recognize.

Hard Fascination—a characteristic of active settings when one watches an energetic activity.

High-Users—those who engage in regular use of green space on campus.

Home Base—a building or other space on a campus map students consider a "home" and visit routinely.

Home Turf—a space that campus users inhabit regularly.

Land Grant Universities—public institutions of higher education designated by a state to receive the benefits of the Morrill Acts of 1862 and 1890.

Low-Users—those who engage in minimal use of green space on campus.

Multiversity—a term that defines a university as having various functions and communities that are brought together within a single academic structure.

Sociofugal—a type of space that keeps people apart, defined by the grid design.

Sociopetal—a type of special design that brings people together, defined by the "radiating star."

Soft Fascination—a characteristic of natural settings when one recovers from directed attention.

Restorative Experience—the idea of escaping the environment that is taxing is at the core of the feeling of being away and could apply to a mental or physical conception of removal. It allows for one to clear their mind.

The City University of New York (CUNY)—the public university system of New York City.

The Serviceman's Readjustment Act (G.I Bill)—a policy that allowed veterans to earn a degree at institutions of higher education across the country.

1 Introduction

Early Historical Context for the American Higher Education System and US Campus Design

Before the republic, higher education in the American colonies relied on the English model at Oxford and Cambridge. Affluent colonial settlers imported educational standards from England that were both traditional and private. However, the late eighteenth century marked the end of the American colonies and the beginning of the American Republic, its strongest commitment to democracy reflected in the desire for a public higher education that could reach its citizenry. Leaving it's Medieval origins behind, this was a system distinct from its private counterparts that had defined higher education in the former American colonies. According to the timeline, the first institutions of public higher education were The University of Georgia and the University of North Carolina at Chapel Hill, chartered within years of each other at the close of the eighteenth century (University of Georgia, 2021). In the American Republic, elitism of the past was replaced by traditions of the future. In the Old World, a university education was usually limited to liberal arts, religious studies, and law yet in the new republic, higher education looked to practical expertise such as engineering and agricultural techniques. In this way, the new Republic valued knowledge that could push the learned working man forward. The history of public higher education in America begins with the Morrill Land-Grant Act of 1862 which used federal funding to build land-grant colleges to serve the common man. Though a defining moment in the democratization of education for less wealthy white men, women and people of color would wait another century to have that same access. To that end, public higher education would continue to transform the country and by extension shape American values. That progressive approach to learning was reflected in its different educational pathways with vocational schools and academic institutions that required two to four years of study. Smaller institutions formed a bridge between high school and postsecondary education. These colleges catered to the academic needs of a community expanding an American higher education system that supported its citizenry. An optimism echoed in the 1947 Truman Commission Report on Higher Education, which emphasized the ways

DOI: 10.4324/9781003130598-1

community colleges could respond to "social problems" and encourage a "fuller realization of democracy" (Zook, 1947, pp. 8–22). In this chapter, the early historical context for the American higher education system and its campus design are explored through the example of Bronx Community College (BCC), a part of the City University of New York (CUNY).

Defining the American Higher Education System

American society is characterized by its complexity and diversity. Its higher education system is a tiered structure that includes senior and junior colleges, with varied programs and disciplinary offerings. These schools are often referred to as two- or four-year colleges, though many two-year colleges offer both academic and professional curricula with very different missions. Those two years of study can lead to an associate degree. Alternately, a two-year college can also result in a transfer to a four-year college and the pursuit of a bachelor's degree. Furthermore, those interested in vocational careers can complete both degree and non-degree certifications at two-year colleges. These distinctive educational pathways support students from diverse backgrounds, with complex identities. The two-year college is further defined by its placement between secondary education and the four-year postsecondary institution. In terms of geographic location, urban, suburban, and rural campuses cater to distinct populations. To understand the origin of these differences, it is crucial to examine the historical background of higher education in America, a past intertwined with the communities it serves.

Brief History of Higher Education in America

In its colonial past, higher education was an exclusive experience for those who could afford private schooling. Harvard University was the first institution of higher education in the new colony; a private college focused on educating sons of elite colonial families. Established in 1636, Harvard was designed in the image of Cambridge University in England, the alma mater of John Harvard. A wealthy clergyman, Harvard died in transit to the New World, bequeathing half his estate, including his library, to the establishment of a prestigious institution that would continue the tradition and culture of academic excellence (Turner, 1990, p. 23). Turner (1990) explains that Peyntree House and its "Cow-Yard" were Harvard's first land starting a trend of referring to university grounds as a yard, eventually replaced by the Greek word "campus" meaning field (p. 23). Similarly, Yale and Princeton were tasked with educating wealthy young men, while those of modest means did not experience widespread access to postsecondary education until Lincoln passed The Morrill Land-Grant Act of 1862. An attempt to unify the divided North and South, The Land-Grant Act ultimately reshaped higher education in the republic. According to Trow during colonial times a college could not exist without a charter administered by the King of England (Trow, 1984, pp. 132–162). Few postsecondary options were available, which made the American Civil War a true turning point in the education system. Essentially, the nineteenth century brought great change. A defining moment in American history, the Land-Grant Act established the public university just as Horace Mann introduced the free common school movement. These innovations in education formed an American system demanding an educated citizenry that could participate in the democratic process as Kaestle (1983) recalls "a sound education would prepare men to vote intelligently" (p. 5). Therefore, under The Land-Grant Act, the federal government allocated money toward the creation of public institutions focused on agricultural sciences and mechanical arts. Ratcliff explains that because of these conditions, the number of state schools increased, establishing a supportive foundation for a citizenry defined by their education (Ratcliff, 1994, p. 6). This expanded the higher education system from being an exclusive experience reserved for the sons of affluent families to one that offered public access and the potential for social mobility. In that way, nineteenth-century America shed its elitist colonial identity for an educated middle class. At the same time, the infrastructure at state schools was often unstable and, despite community support, they lacked sufficient maintenance needed to succeed. In Ratcliff's opinion, the Panic of 1894 assisted in the reform that led to a more defined interpretation of the two-year college, specifically its scope and purpose in society (Ratcliff, 1994, p. 7).

In the early twentieth century, a college education was still neither widely accessible nor a popular path for young men of privilege. As described in *The American College and the Culture of Aspiration, 1915–1940*, Levine (1986) explains that "as late as 1913, fewer than one in twenty young persons attended college and even the most prestigious universities were scrambling to fill their classes . . . admitting many with academic credentials below their stated admissions requirements" (p. 17). It is fair to say that in the period between the two world wars both public and private institutions of higher education underwent a process of rebirth. To that end, institutions began to distinguish themselves in terms of student population, curriculum, and experience, mirroring the social and political shifts that began to shape the country. Levine (1986) clarifies "after World War I, institutions of higher education were no longer content to educate; they set out to train, accredit and impart social status to their students," which marked a distinct alignment between the curriculum and the nation's economy (p. 19).

The Birth of the Community College

Dougherty recounts the birth of the first community college in Joliet, Illinois, in 1901 (Dougherty,1994, p. 115). Reinforcing Ratcliff's analyses on the two-year college's relationship to community and religious support, Dougherty emphasizes the connection between the community college and government. Both authors agree once these colleges were formed, they spread across the country at a rapid pace, though without any uniformity. As stated in *The Junior College Bulletin* in 1919, eleven states offered community colleges with seven in the Midwest, three in the West, and one in the South (Texas) (McDowell, 2015). At that time, US Commissioner of Higher Ed. George Zook explained "it was becoming increasingly apparent that universities and colleges alike (were) beginning to regard the junior college as an institution of great possible usefulness in the field of higher education" (Zook, 1920, p. 2). The Great Depression and New Deal policies had a significant impact on how public higher education developed since the federal government sought ways to combat increasing rates of unemployment. According to Fabricant and Brier, the federal government financially supported the establishment of Emergency Collegiate Centers (ECCs) as early as 1933, prototypical community colleges that provided two years of education for those without jobs while giving work to unemployed teachers and white-collar laborers (Fabricant & Brier, 2016, p. 4).

Science and practical training were also of prime importance to the Roosevelt administration which viewed higher education as an appropriate vehicle to advance the country's defense preparedness. Cardozier recalls the introduction of federally funded research programs in addition to military or nonmilitary programs to train students at universities and colleges, institutions that were consequently experiencing financial hardship (Cardozier, 1993, pp. 211–212). It was apparent that the country's political and social character was reflected in the growth of these institutions. In the aftermath of WWII, with The Serviceman's Readjustment Act of 1944 (The GI Bill), which first reintegrated veterans back into American society by making higher education more accessible and second created affordable housing and trade school (Beach, 2011, p. 75). A planned strategy to transition veterans from service to the workforce, the GI Bill was also a response to the poor reintegration of soldiers in the aftermath of WWI. At community colleges, non-traditional students from working-class backgrounds received an education and upward social mobility. Hence, in 1946, President Truman and George Zook assembled a committee to appraise the state of education in the postwar climate. The President's Commission on Higher Education produced *Higher Education for Democracy* in 1947, a report that articulated their findings and future goals. It supported continued growth in higher education in an effort to keep the country on an upward trajectory. The second wave of community colleges occurred in the sixties, a time when access to higher education widened drastically for America's baby boom generation. This included many previously marginalized populations exemplified by an increase in Black and female enrollment. Colleges were being created at an unprecedented rate to accommodate this rapid growth.

Fittingly, funding became more defined with a desire to make higher education more broadly available to the American public accompanied by increased support from the federal government (Chapman, 2006, p. 35). These changes were the product of the G.I. Bill and movement toward a professionalized population. The Truman Report reinforced the role of community colleges identifying "the first two years of college as a critical period for educating citizens" (Hutchison, 2007, p. 108). To support an infrastructure capable of growth, it recommended that institutions nationwide develop their facilities to accommodate the education of 49 percent of the country's college-aged population, who could benefit from receiving the first two years of a postsecondary education (Chapman, 2006, p. 35). There was great enthusiasm for this plan in that colleges offered entrance to university, which meant universities could establish higher entrance standards in relation to the open admissions policy found at the community college level.

The Impact of the Truman Commission

Brint and Karabel (1989) consider the Truman Commission's role in rebranding the junior college as a community college to emphasize the importance of local ties, also removing the hierarchical relationship that existed between junior and senior colleges (Brint & Karabel, 1989, p. 111). It was previously assumed that students would transfer to a four-year institution once they had completed the first two years at a junior college; however, the fifties introduced the community college as a place that offered a complete education within two years for employment inside the community. The two-year education was recognized as a distinct experience from the traditional four-year school because it involved an intentional focus on learning for a specific purpose that necessitated a tangible amount of time.

As expected, the twentieth century further advanced American institutions with domestic and international events that would precipitate meaningful change such as universal access to public higher education. Prior to the time, little attention had been paid to the two-year college experience, though The President's Commission on Higher Education in 1947 served to establish a clear link between community colleges and the democratization of the American society. Essentially this report mirrored the GI Bill, which largely shaped the relationship between education and the economy by reinforcing the value of postsecondary education to produce semi-skilled or skilled veterans.

Recognizing the heavy burden placed on community colleges with the return of veterans and subsequent increased enrollment, President Truman sought to extend federal support for the two-year college, thus charging a team of civic and educational leaders with the task of examining the system (The President's Commission on Higher Education, 1947, p. 10). The primary focus of this investigation was to better understand both the identity and the functionality of the two-year college. The goal was to expose students to foundational knowledge of the education system in a way that had never been attempted before, thereby further distinguishing the community college's identity in relation to its senior counterparts. The report examined a range of characteristics such as curricula, pathways to increased access, technical programs, and the built environment at community college campuses (The President's Commission on Higher Education, 1947, p. 10). Despite never having completed a postsecondary education, President Truman believed increased access to the community college would open doors to the citizenry and spread the democratic ideals on which the country was founded.

Defining the Community College

In the twentieth century, John Dewey introduced the concept of individual potential, an idea that became the foundation of progressive education. This standard would define the undergraduate experience of higher education as Dewey (1966) asserts "utility, culture, information, preparation for social efficiency, mental discipline or power" are the cornerstones of a college education (p. 446). Likewise, Brint and Karabel (1989) explain "the mission of the junior college is to democratize the elite postsecondary system in the United States by creating multiple access points for underserved students" (p. 9). It is this sense of purpose and idealism that has defined the community college. Although from a historical perspective its function has changed as Levine describes how in the 1920s the two-year college was "a program designed to provide students from different backgrounds with the opportunity to reach an acceptable level of academic achievement by the end of their second year" (Levine, 1986, p. 99). Separating colleges into junior and senior levels was a proposed solution to the attrition experienced at many four-year schools while creating a bridge from postsecondary education into college. Moreover, the two-year college is very distinct from the traditional four-year institution because it reflects the class differences embedded in American society. Inequalities that emerge at high school, evolve at college and later define the workforce.

The community college is a space where democratic ideals and class structure collide. It is because of this unique position in the education system, the two-year college is expected to offer opportunity and access while creating pathways to higher levels of education and the workforce. During the interwar period, Levine recalls the junior college was originally seen as "the people's college," an institution that could reach the working-class citizen, though, for many, systemic inequalities would continue to hamper upward mobility (Levine, 1986, p. 163). An example of this is open admissions at two year institutions, a policy that establishes greater access to higher education. However there are other mechanisms in place that can serve to limit opportunity for advancement in this complex system such as language proficiency and remediation programs. Ideally these programs bridge the knowledge gap, yet for many they can become potential barriers that cloud the path to graduation and beyond.

Clark refers to that very process of sorting and selecting which naturally occurs at two year institutions as the *Cool Out*. It is a term that defines an institutional culture of setting low expectations for community college students by implementing a set of informal practices to manage students who are either caught in the achievement gap or lack the fundamental resources to complete a degree. In "The 'Cooling-Out' Function in Higher Education," he argues that the student's goal of completing a degree is equal to the desire for upward mobility to managerial positions within the class structure, while their reality is entry-level positions in the workforce upon graduation (Clark, 1960, p. 513). He identifies the social factors which contribute to disparate conditions that exist at various levels of higher education and extend directly to the labor market. Consequently, Levine discusses a similar experience between 1915 and 1940, when the culture of aspiration stimulated an unprecedented demand for higher education of any kind, a symbol of economic and social mobility (Levine, 1986, p. 21). The national trend for attending postsecondary institutions was pronounced by the sixties. It was also met by a favorable response from the federal government which increased funding for two-year colleges at the close of the decade and into the seventies.

As highlighted by Mertins and Brandt (1979), the government shifted from supplying a mere 6 percent of revenue to 8.4 percent under the Nixon administration, which indicated a deep support for these institutions, specifically their rate of growth across the country. The seventies brought a familiar optimism for the community college since the government imagined it as a place where citizens could receive an occupational training, diverting students away from the traditional four-year education. Effectively, the community college was adopted as a symbol of educational reform, whereby a liberal arts education was exchanged for a vocational one that had a practical curriculum.

This is further reiterated in The Higher Education Act of 1972, which stressed the importance of training or retraining people for positions that required various forms of skilled labor "but excluding any program to prepare individuals for employment in occupations . . . to be generally considered professional or which require[d] advanced training" (p. 192). At that time, the landscape in higher education was geared toward an inclusive design that sought to elevate enrollment and bolster confidence in the nontraditional college experience. The federal government actively supported its citizenry in continuing their educational goals into secondary education, purposeful and aligned with a specific function in the labor market. During this period the vocational education was of prime importance and new language was introduced. The Higher Education Act of 1972 encouraged the term "postsecondary occupational education" in addition to replacing the junior college for the two-year college, to lessen the divisive hierarchy embedded in the higher education system (p. 192).

How the College Functions

Beach (2011) contends higher education policy in the United States was established on "two politicized myths: *socioeconomic meritocracy* and *equal access to higher education*" in that just as the number and type of community colleges have increased over time, so too has the level of inequality (p. xix). The author is critical of the community college's role in American society because the cornerstones of this institution are open-access and low cost. The author counters commercial rhetoric on the college's origins being egalitarian, asserting the community college was in fact supposed to limit access to higher education. However, that gatekeeper function was disrupted by the political uprisings of the sixties and seventies. Thus, it was progressive notions regarding access that ultimately rebranded it as a pathway to higher education. Beach (2011) references the president of Stanford University, who described the junior college as "an open institution that would allow new generations of students to 'try out' higher education 'without great economic disadvantage and without leaving home after high school graduation'" (p. 5).

Between the early and mid-twentieth century, the community college allowed high school graduates to continue their education, yet it would also become a place where previously marginalized students were introduced to higher education. Fifty percent of students were enrolled in a two-year college by the close of the twentieth century and 41 percent were identified as being minority students (Beach, 2011, p. 7).

Policy and Funding

Decision-making at the community college is largely accomplished at the state and local level. A combination of state and local funding contributes to the operating expenses of public institutions of higher education. The Tenth Amendment of the Constitution granted the state responsibility for education, therefore funding at the federal level, is secondary to the governing state's contribution, with additional funds derived from local government. According to the National Archives, the Tenth Amendment declares "[t]he powers not delegated to the United States by the Constitution, nor prohibited by it to the States, are reserved to the States respectively, or to the people," which means the states assume power of education by default (National Archives, 2018). The relationship between state funding and the evolution of the community college dates back to the early twentieth century. The Facilities Inventory and Classification Manual explains "State agencies, with both governing and coordinating functions, have the responsibility to recommend the most efficient and effective use of scarce state and institutional resources, as well as to minimize the cost burden on students and their parents" (National Center for Education Statistics, 2006). This process requires the utilization of comprehensive research and accurate analytic tools to assess these seemingly disparate needs.

Dougherty clarifies the state initially started to engage in the development of the community college system by granting localities permission if they met certain conditions. First to introduce such legislation was California in 1907 while New York was slow to follow suit, with compliance in 1948 and its first community college opening in the fifties (Dougherty, 1994, p. 145). By the sixties, direct funding was allocated by the state directly to colleges, many allowing enrollment to contribute to the allotment of funds. In Smith's view, the massive development of physical space at American community colleges during the sixties and seventies ended by the close of the seventies, leaving most colleges to maintain their existing campuses, while at the same time accommodating ever-increasing enrollment (Smith's, 1994, p. 355). At the same time, Egginton highlights some regulations indirectly disenfranchise community college students such as designating a percentage of state and federal aid to full-time students at four-year colleges. In *The Splintering of the American Mind*, he stresses more than 40 percent of the country's 18 million college students attend community colleges, not four-year institutions, which makes the crisis of funding and space constraints more pressing than ever (Egginton, 2018, p. 137).

Policies of Space

The mid-twentieth century introduced the highest rate of growth in terms of campuses throughout the country. The G.I. Bill and the Civil Rights movement triggered an unprecedented increase in college attendance that was composed of veterans, women, and people of color. The federal government offered institutions of higher education funding to develop research in the science and technology fields that would allow the country to match the advancement taking place in the Soviet Republic. It was a matter of national defense. In *Campuses in Cities: Places Between Engagement and Retreat*, Blaik (2007) suggests that the exceptional cash infusion to the university "coincided with a wave of urban-renewal polices that focused on slum clearance, and an era that promoted a style of brutal and modern architecture obsessed with technology, order, and hierarchy" (pp. 1–2). These changes impacted the physical landscape with design choices harmful to the functionality and aesthetic of the urban environment. He posits the university was presented with two challenges that included methods of integration within preexisting urban spaces in addition to honoring the concept of an academic oasis that could offer a scholar respite from the challenges of the city. The design choices made at urban campuses across the country were likely influenced by the obstacle of expanding within a densely built environment.

The aftermath of WWII brought on a period of exceptional growth in America that extended from industry to the large university. Kerr coined the term *multiversity*, a university that had various functions and communities that were brought together within this single academic structure (Kerr, 1963, p. 1). Postwar policies were geared toward rapid growth and initiated by President Roosevelt in 1944. The goal was to increase access to resources such as housing and education, producing unprecedented levels of prosperity both educational and professional, which would also translate into intergenerational wealth for white Americans from the middle class.

A Bronx Tale: The Community College

In 1957, The City University of New York established its second community college in University Heights, a neighborhood located in the Bronx. Like Brooklyn and Queen's first senior colleges, this campus was the product of a decade of effort by civic-minded groups in Bronx County to meet the growing need for increased higher education facilities in the "Borough of Universities and Progress" (BCC, 2018b). The first president of the college was Dr. Morris Meister, who guided the new school through its early years, although during the fiscal crisis of the seventies New York experienced tremendous upheaval across its five boroughs. The prosperity of the previous two decades was attributed to the postwar expansion policies that gave veterans access to the housing market and educational institutions. Similarly, the Civil Rights movement provided increased access to historically disadvantaged communities. Glazer (1987) recalls:

> CUNY missed the golden age of the sixties when college construction was booming everywhere, and campuses were being overbuilt. A recalcitrant Legislature and an unsympathetic Governor, all because of an anachronism—free tuition, stunted its growth. The environment would have been different today if it had moved faster and had assured the state more of a role in its development.
>
> (p. 257)

In contrast, the seventies shifted the country into a period of social and economic chaos. It was a time when "firehouses closed, mass transit stalled, libraries shut their doors, school class sizes swelled, routine services like garbage collection became unpredictable, and thousands of would-be students found themselves shut out of CUNY because the university simply stopped processing their applications" (Fein-Phillips, 2013). During this moment of fragility, local people campaigned to protect public resources such as CUNY colleges located in the boroughs that were threatened with closure due to the economic downturn.

The Master Plan

Amid the fiscal crisis, New York University (NYU) decided to consolidate its campus to downtown Manhattan, where they already occupied property in Greenwich Village that surrounded Washington Square Park. To that end, their engineering and polytechnic campus located in University Heights became available when NYU sold the site to the State Dormitory Authority in July of 1973, "providing the College with a desperately needed central campus facility" (Bronx Community College, 2018a). The new landscape encompassed a 50-acre space that afforded tranquility and historic qualities of a traditional campus environment, where the academic community could engage in scholarly pursuits. The BCC Master Plan of 1975–1980 identifies the expanse of its greenery that is "lined by trees in the southwest corner of the campus . . . natural areas that will provide the faculty and students with areas of repose where they can find places of quiet and solitude and meditation, study or casual conversation" (BCC, 2018a). BCC is the only college in the State of New York that is designated as a National Historical Landmark that pays tribute to its collection of architecturally significant buildings, making it one of the largest and historic campuses within the CUNY system (BCC, 2018b).

Negotiation

Donal Farley, Assistant to the first Vice-Chancellor for Campus Planning and Development, began working in the CUNY Central Office in 1967. He was also one of three individuals assigned to participate in the appraisal of the New York University (NYU) Heights campus in 1972. In an interview, he recalls the turbulence of the seventies created great challenges for NYU's campus in the Heights, with dwindling enrollment rates (Farley, 2019). This NYU campus was then known as the College of Arts and Science and the School of Engineering. It offered an undergraduate education starting in 1894 and continued until its decline in the early seventies, a time of widespread financial hardship in New York.

The fiscal crisis of the seventies permitted NYU to lobby the State to bail them out in 1972 and legislation, in turn, allowed the City University of New York to purchase their campus. An appraisal of the NYU campus was requested on behalf of both institutions to determine an appropriate price for the purchase of the campus. Farley reminisces about the request made by the mediating lawyer, McGrath, for each party to write an amount they would be willing to pay on a piece of paper. That amount was determined to be a little higher than 60 million dollars, a figure that naturally bothered NYU's team, due to the forty-million-dollar difference in their proposed estimate. Farley recounts when McGrath was later asked about how he arrived at the final figure, he simply replied "magic," creating a permanent campus for BCC (Farley, 2019).

The Campus

To appreciate the evolution of higher education in the United States is to understand the origins of public education and the importance of access. A product of America's growing pains, the community college embodies those ideals of democracy and revolution. Policy, conflict, and social change are features of this story, though it would not be complete without a conversation on space. In present day, issues such as urban renewal have altered the lived experience of many residents across communities and neighborhoods. This has compromised widespread access, instead replacing it with complex challenges to public higher education, particularly for those who come from historically disadvantaged communities. With those ideas in mind, the following exploration of the built and lived environment will be realized at Bronx Community College, one of the earliest additions to the City University of New York.

References

Beach, J. M. (2011). *Gateway to opportunity: A history of the community college in the United States*. Sterling, VA: Stylus Publishing.

Blaik, O. (2007). Campuses in cities: Places between engagement and retreat. *The Chronicle of Higher Education, 53*(25), 25.

Brint, S., & Karabel, J. (1989). *The Diverted Dream: Community Colleges and the Promise of Educational Opportunities in America, 1900–1985*. New York, NY: Oxford Press.

Bronx Community College. (2018a). *1975–1980 Bronx Community College comprehensive plan. Master plans*. Retrieved from www.bcc.cuny.edu/faculty-staff/campus-facilitiesplanning/master-plans/ (accessed November 24, 2018).

Bronx Community College. (2018b). *History and architecture. How the college started*. Retrieved from www.bcc.cuny.edu/about-bcc/history-architecture/ (accessed November 24, 2018).

Cardozier, V. R. (1993). *Colleges and universities in World War II*. Westport, CT: Praeger.

Chapman, P. (2006). *American Places: In Search of the Twenty-first Century Campus*. Westport, CT: Praeger.

Clark, B. R. (1960). The "Cooling-Out" function in higher education. *The American Journal of Sociology, 65*(6), 569–576.

Dewey, J. (1966). *Democracy and education*. New York, NY: Free Press.

Dougherty, K. (1994). *The contradictory college. The conflicting origins, impacts, and futures of the community college*. Albany, NY: State University of New York Press.

Education Amendments Act of 1972, 20 U.S.C. §§1681–1688 (2018).

Egginton, W. (2018). *The splintering of the American mind: Identity politics, inequality, and community in today's college campuses*. New York, NY: Bloomsbury.

Fabricant, M., & Brier, S. (2016). *Austerity blues: Fighting for the soul of public higher education*. Baltimore, MD: Johns Hopkins University Press.

Farley, D. personal communication, April 4, 2019.

Fein-Phillips, K. (2013, April 6). The legacy of the fiscal crisis. *The Nation*. https://www.thenation.com/article/society/bloody-flags/

Glazer, J. (1987). *A case of the decision in 1976 to initiate tuition for matriculated undergraduate students in the City University of New York*. PhD dissertation, New York University.

Hutchison, P. A. (2007). The Truman Commission's vision of the future. *Thought & Action*, 107–115.

Kaestle, C. F. (1983). *Pillars of the republic: Common schools and American society, 1780-1860*. New York, NY: Hill and Wang.

Kerr, C. (1963). *The uses of the university*. Cambridge, MA: Harvard University Press.

Levine, D. O. (1986). *The American College and the culture of aspiration, 1915–1940*. Ithaca, NY: Cornell University.

McDowell, F. (2015). *Department of the Interior Bureau of Education. Bulletin, 1919, Number 35. The Junior College*. Amsterdam. Netherlands. Leopold Classic Library.

Mertins, P. E., & Brandt, N. J. (1979). *Financial statistics of institutions of higher education: current funds revenues and expenditures*. Washington, DC: National Center for Educational Statistics.

National Archives. (2018). *The bill of rights: A transcription*. Retrieved from www.archives.gov/founding-docs/bill-of-rights-transcript (accessed January 9, 2019).

National Center for Education Statistics. (2006). *Postsecondary education. Facilities inventory and classification manual*. Retrieved from https://nces.ed.gov/pubs2006/ficm/index.asp (accessed December 1, 2018).

President's Commission on Higher Education. (1947). *Higher education for American democracy: a report of the President's Commission on Higher Education*. Washington: U.S. Govt.

Ratcliff, J. L. (1994). Seven streams in the historical development of the modern American community college. In G. Baker (Ed.), *A handbook on the community college in America: Its history, mission and management* (pp. 3–14). Westport, CT: Greenwood Publishing.

Smith, R. K. (1994). Building budgets for effective resource utilization. In G. Baker (Ed.), *A handbook on the community college in America: Its history, mission and management* (pp. 350–358). Westport, CT: Greenwood Publishing.

Trow, M. A. (1984). The analysis of status. In B. R. Clark (Ed.), *Perspectives in higher education* (pp. 132–162). Berkeley, CA: University of California Press.

Turner, P. V. (1990). *Campus: An American planning tradition*. Cambridge, MA: The MIT Press.

University of Georgia. (2021). *About UGA*. Retrieved from www.uga.edu (accessed November 20, 2020).

Zook, G. F. (1922). *National Conference of Junior Colleges, 1920 and first annual meeting of American Association of Junior Colleges, 1921*. Washington, DC: United States Government Printing Office.

Zook, G. F. (1947). *Higher education for American democracy: A report of the President's Commission on higher education*. Washington, DC: United States Government Printing Office.

2 The Interaction Between Learning Space and Experience

Wellbeing, Belonging, and Scholarly Identity

In the *Genius Loci: Towards a Phenomenology of Architecture*, Norberg-Schulz (1979) suggests "everyday experience tells us different actions need different environments to take place in a satisfactory way" (p. 8). That sentiment is realized in Thomas Jefferson's concept of the *academical village* or an ideal learning environment, a sacred space embodied by thoughtful campus design. The campus design at the University of Virginia personifies Jeffereson's vision. Similarly for Turner (1990) the *academical village* "summarizes the basic trait of American higher education from the colonial period to the twentieth century: the conception of colleges and universities as cities in microcosm" (p. 3). To appreciate campus as a place, this chapter will explore historic and social aspects of the learning environment at an urban public institution.

Campus as Place

Campus design curates an experience that dates back to Ancient Greece and Rome, when Socrates and Plato imagined an oasis for learning situated beyond the metropolis. Tranquility was essential in this setting since it allowed for reflection, abstraction and debate. Knowledge was produced by individuals and ideas. To that end, in the American colonies, early universities were modeled on medieval English schools at Oxford and Cambridge. Strategically placed away from urban distraction these schools increased the opportunity for contemplation, fundamental to scholarly identity. Turner (1990) recalls the monastic origins of the English education system in the cloistered built environment, which led to the introduction of the enclosed quadrangle (p. 10). The author emphasizes the relationship between land use, safety, and control. He cites the "whoring and disorder" in Oxford as a reason for students later being required to live on campus as of 1410 (Turner, 1990, p. 10). A mandate that produced the quadrangle, a design concept created for residence on campus. England imagined the campus as a place where a community of scholars could congregate to exchange ideas and share a common academic experience. The campus offered both sanctuary and respite from the outside world.

In *The Medieval University: Oxford and Cambridge to 1500*, Cobban suggests in a European context, the twelfth- and fourteenth-century *universitas* was devoted to craft guilds and municipal councils that served as corporate bodies. It was not until the late nineteenth century that the university became its own separate entity that was distinct from other modes of organization (Cobban, 1988, p. 2). Before the fifteenth century, the university was known as a *stadium generale*, *stadium* being a school focused on advanced studies and *generale* referring to students who came from a broad area (Cobban, 1988, p. 2). This contrasted with the *stadium particulaire* that catered to the academic needs of a town or a specific area. Oxford and Cambridge were intentionally established outside the urban locale, unlike other universities of the time in Bologna, Paris, and Montpellier. These medieval English universities were very intentionally placed in the countryside because cities were prone to the natural urban disturbances (Cobban, 1988, p. 7). Hence in the New World, Turner (1990) claims "the romantic notion of the college in nature, removed from the erupting forces of the city, became an American ideal" (p. 4).

Early U.S. Campus Formations

According to Chapman (2006), the Olmsted Report on campus design included "arrangements designed to favorably affect the habits and inclinations of students and to qualify them for a wise and beneficent exercise of the rights and duties of citizens and shareholders" (p. 25). The American colonies saw the first insititution of higher education with the establishment of Harvard University in 1636 located in the Massachusetts Bay Colony, an academic experience reserved for the social elite. Chapman considers that sense of place at the early campuses of Harvard and Yale, including a village commons at the center, a stylistic quality derived from the English campus. Expansive green spaces were integral in unifying various buildings devoted to housing or academic instruction (Chapman, 2006, p. 26). Thomas Jefferson's notion of the *academical village* emphasized community; one that fostered meaningful exchange between faculty and student. He envisioned an environment that offered a unique academic experience. In *American Places*, Chapman (2006) reiterates the importance of this historic period stating, "in his quest to build a regional public academy in central Virginia, Jefferson would play a seminal role in shaping the American campus as we know it today" (p. 3). It was here, Jefferson fused his passion for architectural design with a desire to nurture the scholarly experience. In this way, he aimed to combine the beauty of this rural landscape with the sensibilities of the urban environment. Similarly, Hiss (1990) explores the role of environment in the belief that

> places have an impact on our sense of self, our sense of safety, the kind of work we get done, the ways we interact with other people, even our ability to function as citizens in a democracy. In short, the places where we spend our time affect the people we are and can become.
>
> (p. xii)

Space for Intellectual Exchange

Saltrick (1996) discusses the college experience as a vital component to higher education, stressing

> college for many of us is a process of socialization, a rite of passage, which requires its own material culture ... places on campus where students connect with one another. The strength of the future physical university lies less in pure information and more in college as community.
>
> (p. 31)

Simply put, the campus should support both academic and personal growth. Saltrick (1996) suggests that design should cultivate a feeling of connectivity to prevent isolation meaning "place making has to be human in scale, rich in texture, and abundant in spatial serendipity" (p. 31). Implicit in campus design is the exchange of ideas. Adequate space is essential for optimal learning in an environment that caters to both the mind and the body, a place where community supports the individual.

Wellbeing

Once reserved for men of means, today a postsecondary education has become a rite of passage for the average American student. Yet in its early form, the university experience involved the retreat of wealthy young white men to historic buildings situated in serene settings. Places where the mind and body were carefully sculpted by other more learned people. And over time, industrialization, urban expansion, and population growth translated that idealized notion of the academic environment to something more conducive to modern life, one that was less remote and more accessible. The traditional university was reborn. Alternate versions appeared to meet new and different needs, for example, the two- and four-year college. Urban, suburban, and rural institutions were established just as for-profit, private, and public nonprofit schools were introduced. At present, increased access to education and rapid modernization produced an urban community college experience where campus life is balanced with responsiblities at work and home.

The Center for Community College Research (CCRC) indicates that 5.5 million students were enrolled in public two-year colleges in the United States in the fall of 2019 with 1.9 million full-time students. To that extent, the term nontraditional student is far less accurate today since older students comprise a significant portion of the student population with little division between college, employment, and home. Furthermore, demographic information from the CCRC states in 2015–2016, 37 percent of students who were dependent came from families that generate an annual income of less than $20,000 (CCRC, 2021). According to statistics from the 2018 academic year, community colleges represented an undergraduate population that was 55 percent Hispanic, 44 percent Black, 45 percent Asian, and 42 percent White in comparison to the general student population across the United States, which means more than half of any ethnic group is likely to attend community college (CCRC, 2021). From that data, it is apparent these institutions are educating a significant portion of the American population. In that way, for some students, the community college is the first step toward a four-year degree while for others it is the last step before entering the workforce. Regardless an education at the community college level should attend to the experiential components of an ideal learning environment. Engagement with nature, solitude, and serenity are possible when wellbeing is considered an integral part of success. Historically, natural settings have defined more traditional campuses and have also attended to that concept of wellness by removing users from the confines of everyday life. This is an important observation in terms of the community college experience because students can benefit from a campus setting that values their ability to both recover and connect to others.

Relatedly, McFarland et al. (2008) note "researchers have found that students' perception of their overall academic experience and the campus environment is related to academic accomplishment" (p. 232). In their study of the relationship between undergraduate students use of campus green spaces and perceptions of quality of life, they used an online survey to assess experience on campus (McFarland et al., 2008, p. 232). In addition, Kaplan's (1995) Attention Restoration Theory (ART) proposes the concept of directed attention and fascination, developed from James' concept of voluntary/effortful attention versus involuntary/effortless attention. Essentially, the author asserts directed attention is needed to step back from a situation in order to assess what is happening. This allows one to process and plan information, though after a prolonged period of time one also becomes fatigued (Kaplan, 1995, p. 171). ART suggests that fascination (effortless attention) pauses directed attention and allows for recovery. It includes two distinct types of fascination, namely *hard* which is experienced by watching energetic activity like racecar driving versus *soft* such as observing visuals or merely taking a walk in a natural setting. Fortunately, natural environments are particularly rich in the characteristics necessary for fascination to occur, the foundation to restorative experience. Recovery from directed attention is possible during soft fascination because reflection can be restorative. These are important experiential qualities to consider in the design of a community college campus.

Reactions and Perceptions

Speake et al. (2013) address the relationship between positive student experience and contact with green space on campus. In their assessment of green space, they explore student preferences between manicured or naturalistic green areas. Their findings reveal that campus space is used for social and athletic activities that contribute to a richer academic experience with reduced stress levels as 81 percent of students report having a distinct and favorite place on campus (Speake et al., 2013, p. 25). Similarly, Cooper-Marcus and Wischemann propose campus design can influence mental health and emotional wellbeing, a phenomenon they explored by investigating how students of environmental design perceived the physical space on campus at Berkeley (Cooper-Marcus & Wischemann, 1998, p. 179).

This research targeted the student experience inside and outside campus buildings. Participants were asked to share word associations to define their feelings about these spaces on campus. Feedback on inside spaces contained language such as "enclosed, bored, frustrated, and anxious" whereas outside felt "quiet, calm, relaxed, peaceful, green and comfortable" (Cooper-Marcus & Wischemann, 1998, p. 179). For the authors, these words indicate buildings embody expectation, a sense of duty in relation to work, study, and lecture (Cooper-Marcus & Wischemann, 1998, p. 179). This research studies place and state of mind, as students can interpret their surroundings in ways that compound or alleviate challenging aspects of the learning experience.

College requires the development of somewhat contradictory identities because in an academic community, students are expected to be independent learners and social beings. The most prominent features of the learning experience embrace the acquisition of knowledge, the process of reflection, the development of a scholarly identity, and the feeling of belonging. In Naidoo's (2020) view, campus design shapes those aspects of the learning experience because access to space that is both green and shared can ease the stress of being a student. These spaces offer respite in the academic environment, locations where students can engage with the outdoors either alone or with others. Cooper-Marcus and Wischemann (1998) introduced the term *front yard*, because "for some people the idea of sunbathing or relaxing in a public space may be inhibiting, but resting, meditating, or daydreaming in a familiar place that feels like one's *home base*, around people one knows or recognizes, may be more acceptable" on campus (p. 181).

Their research also identifies the concept of *home turf*, a place users return to regularly because it is familiar, a campus space where others go to eat, relax, or converse. (Cooper-Marcus & Wischemann, 1998, p. 181). Frequent use cultivates a sense of belonging at the home turf. Accordingly, the pedestrian nature of the campus encourages people to feel they can move freely through these spaces and return to them for a social or private outdoor experience. The *backyard* is a second space that is designated for faculty, staff, and students. It is defined by its three-sided enclosure, a notable feature of Oxford and Cambridge, where private spaces support more intimate encounters between smaller groups of people talking or eating on campus. Shared campus space located behind a building increases the effect of a cozy or quiet atmosphere, one that is exclusively available to members of the campus community. Cooper-Marcus and Wischemann (1998) refer to these interactions on campus as "collegial encounters," expressing the intentional configuration of space that encourages fraternization between people in outside spaces on campus (p. 183). More traditional campus design tends to incorporate opportunities for engagement with people within intimate areas such as inward-facing quadrangles, gardens, and diverse landscapes with seating that is spaced out.

Politics of Privacy

In *Privacy and the Bathroom*, Chapin (1951) discovered,

> privacy is needed for thinking, reflection, reading, study, for the aesthetic enjoyment and contemplation. Intrusions on the fulfillment of personal desires need to be shut off to avoid the internal tensions that are built up from the frustrations, resentments and the irritations of multiple contacts with others.
>
> (p. 840)

With that in mind, privacy is especially important at the community college, which traditionally serves students from historically disadvantaged communities. Here access to green space is very much a social justice issue since community college students often occupy multiple identities such as sole breadwinners of a low-income household, undocumented or first-generation college student, as well as resident of a neighborhood that is underserved. Chapin (1951) argues, the role of privacy goes beyond physical and emotional aspects of being alone because "there is often a need to escape from the compulsions of one's social role, to be able to retire from the role of the parent, spouse, relative or child, as the case may be" (p. 840). Privacy becomes a vital component in the process of contemplation, reprieve, and renewal.

Therefore, the domestic environment mirrors the academic landscape in that physical space can translate to mental space. In this study, Chapin uncovers the social aspects of privacy. He notes that in a wealthier home some conduct is reserved for private settings since there is an abundance of space to accommodate different needs. Conversely, in working-class homes, all space is shared, and privacy is rarely experienced, which means all manner of conduct takes place in the public realm. During his study, he found that wealthy female participants, who had always had their own bedroom or bathroom were shocked by bathroom sharing schedules used by girls from middle-class households. Similarly, those women from working-class households were surprised a schedule was even needed to share space because they came from homes where sharing was a natural part of cohabitation.

This is not unlike university choice as every year upper middle-class students shop for the right campus fit visiting multiple schools to find the one that best fits their personal needs. On the other hand, students from lower-income backgrounds often make their decision based on practicality such as cost and distance from work or home. The feel of an environment and an assessment of what a space has to offer are aspects of preference inherently tied to social class. In *Distinction* (1984), Bourdieu states

> the dominant class constitutes a relatively autonomous space whose structure is defined by the distribution of economic and social capital among its members, each class fraction being categorized by a certain configuration of this distribution to which there corresponds a certain lifestyle.
>
> (p. 260)

He acknowledges how social class frames choice and preference. In that regard, students from higher social classes feel empowered to choose the campus that provides the best experience, while students from lower social classes will likely accept the campus that offers both value and convenience since affordability is a primary concern.

With defining features of the campus design in mind, Boyer's (1987) research on the undergraduate experience suggests, "students need solitude and intimacy as well as togetherness; and they should be able to choose their companions without institutional constraint" (p. 187). Jacobs (1961) explores this notion in her discussion of urban life, stating, "privacy is a precious commodity in the city. It is indispensable . . . it is precious and indispensable everywhere but most places you cannot get it" (p. 58). She identifies the illusive nature of solitude in urban space, where contemplation and disengagement are seldom possible. For the urban community college student, the campus may offer their first encounter with privacy in an academic setting. A profound opportunity to seek sanctuary in the quietness of thoughts or to ruminate on new information. The author underscores planning the experience of space. She mentions that city residential planning nurtures an experience with others that supports people of means, where the disadvantaged are simply reminded of their limited choices in the lived environment (Jacobs, 1961, p. 65). The challenges of an urban context are often mirrored in its social institutions, places less conducive to focus and concentration, which are needed for learning.

Private Versus Public

Likewise, Edward T. Hall (1969) explores the difference between public and private spaces highlighting the control humans have over their environment, through architecture, planning, and design. He posits that "man is now in the position of actually creating the total world he lives in, what ethologists refer to as biotype" hence, man is the architect of the kind of organism he will become (p. 4). By extension, Hall proposes the way cities are designed to include neighborhoods intricately connected by concrete or trees, will in turn produce different kinds of people. He makes specific reference to public institutions such as mental hospitals and prisons as well as the contrast in space experienced between suburbs and slums.

The congestion found in New York is unparalleled by any other city in North America. Overcrowding has become a distinct feature of the urban lifestyle that defines city life, though some communities experience it more acutely than others. Access to natural landscapes is less common though they offer a welcomed distraction from the pollution and noise found in densely populated areas. Public parks and tree lined streets provide a cost-free connection to nature, allowing people to engage with restorative environments while living in a fast-paced city where the measure of success is high productivity.

Hall (1969) explains that "man's sense of space is closely related to his sense of self, which is an intimate transaction with his environment," an observation that implies the importance of restorative places, central to ideal living conditions (p. 63). He also discussus, he discusses, Humphrey Osmond's study of cultural proxemics, which identifies two types of space, namely *sociofugal* that keeps people apart and *sociopetal* that tends to bring people together (Hall, 1969, p. 108). While conducting research in a psychiatric hospital in Saskatchewan, Osmond observed certain spaces illicit specific behaviors in terms of movement and the desire to convene or retreat from the group. Some examples include the waiting room at a railway station versus the configuration of tables at a French sidewalk café. Within this dialogue exists a deeper statement on the uses of space or what Hall (1969) refers to as the "dynamism of space, how a person's perception of a space is related to action or what can be done in a given space—rather than what is seen by passive viewing" (p. 115).

The concept of gathering and scattering can be applied to urban planning, more specifically public transportation. Hall contends that the transit system of Paris and Spain are *sociopetal* in nature because a "radiating star" brings commuters together at central points in their journey. Unlike the *sociofugal* design of the "grid" used in England, which contains a series of separated points that spread both people and places as it extends (Hall, 1969, p. 146). These are useful observations when thinking about the relationship between urban design, public transportation and shared space, like an urban campus. A fast-paced city like New York operates within a "grid" system that naturally produces divisions between public and private space based on power, privilege and status. Public institutions such the urban community college are locations where both sociopetal and sociofugal design principles co-exist. In *Designing Places for People* (1985), Deasy and Laswell examine how friendship formation and group membership are formed in a public space. The author highlights that "if there is a place to stand outside the flow of traffic, or even better a comfortable place to sit down, social contact develops. If this kind of event recurs regularly, a social center is born" (Deasy and Lasswell, 1985, p. 129).

The ideal learning environment should be a respite from the urban jungle. Particularly at the urban community college that caters to students who identify as immigrants, lower-income, non-native English speakers, and academically underprepared high school graduates. These issues are further addressed in *Beyond the Melting Pot*, where Glazer and Moynihan (1970) argue major ethnic groups can maintain distinct identities for generations, despite design choices related to housing and planning that often do not factor preservation of those identities (p. 166). With that in mind, design choices at the community college can overlook distinct indentities within its student population, a social justice issue that highlights a lack of institutional support.

Belonging

The college experience is equally a social and academic experience, both to success. Murphy and Zirkel (2015) remind us that "a sense of belonging is socially constructed, informed by a student's experiences in a particular educational context." The challenges of "fitting in" are likely mitigated by time spent engaging with people and places in the academic landscape. According to Walton and Cohen (2007), "if social belonging is important to intellectual achievement, members of historically excluded ethnic groups may suffer a disadvantage." Alternately, Cooper-Marcus and Wischemann (1987) propose that students have spaces on campus they identify as home base or "a home away from home," places where they feel the most comfortable (p. 177). Such places tend to help orient students in their routine of attending class, reviewing course material, socializing with others, or simply reflecting on ideas. Their methods included behavior trace analysis, activity mapping, and formal interviews.

First, behavior trace analysis required students to identify past behavior that indicated common areas they frequented while on campus. By recalling habitual movement on campus, students were able to describe various ways they engaged with space. This method was appropriate for the Berkeley study because students could reflect on their lived experience of campus design. Second, through activity mapping students were able to indicate a variety of spaces on campus such as *favorite spaces* and home turf. The activity mapping required a random sample of students to indicate which building or other space on a campus map they consider a home building or base. This process revealed a preference for green or natural spaces that were not necessarily the home turf or territory of any specific building. Favorite spaces were selected based on a range of criteria such as naturalness and open space, peace and quiet, shade or sun, people watching and proximity to water (Cooper-Marcus, 1987, p. 178). Additionally, as defined by students' natural elements comprised, grass, shrubs, and trees. Activities that took place at favorite spaces offered both social and restorative experiences. Students identified talking, eating, people watching, meditating, and playing Frisbee as some of the standard ways in which they spend time in outdoor spaces on campus. Of the 400 respondents, the study reports that 90 percent had a home base on campus. An expected result for graduate students, faculty, and employees who likely have an office, desk, or a department on campus, though it proved equally true for undergraduates, indicating a psychological desire for a home away from home.

Germane to this study is a discussion of belonging and experience, highlighted by Marcus and Wischemann's notion of the front porch, which describes outdoor spaces that lead directly into frequented buildings such as departments or common areas. The authors suggest the front porch addresses both the physical and psychological aspects that characterize public and private space, offering cues to transition from one type of behavior to another, depending on location. Based on their research at Berkeley, the authors state

> the need to feel that one belongs to one spot is so compelling that most students, even those with no formal tie to any single building (i.e., those who had not yet chosen a major) still appropriated a place to which they returned daily.
>
> (Cooper-Marcus, 1987, p. 177)

Their findings imply that students develop a sense of belonging by establishing a home base in their campus routine because it allows them to construct a community within the academic environment that puts them at ease and makes them feel welcome. A second term utilized is the concept of "home turf."

Belonging and Restorative Experience

Kaplan and Kaplan (1982) speak of "a continuum of clarity and chaos that exist and influence patterns of fascination and chaos" which they believe is influenced by the degree of harmony that exists between one's purpose and their environment (p. 114). In an educational setting, a student's sense of belonging in a space can impact their emotional range. The learning experience is composed of intellectual challenges, social interaction, and periods of isolation. In this case, the academic institution can make users feel integrated within a larger collective. At a college campus, comfort is achieved at formal and informal gatherings in the academic landscape. On campuses where large spaces exist for faculty and students to roam within greenery and trees, the need to explore those spaces will be heightened, if users feel they are integrated within that environment. According to Kaplan and Kaplan, the degree of uncertainty one faces is a product of the known aspect of the present and the ambiguity of the future.

The authors examine restorative environments concentrating on the desire for escape that accompanies heightened levels of stress and the calming effect of nature. Stress is defined as the "preparation for an anticipated event that has been evaluated as being threatening or harmful" though they also leave room for the possibility that stress can occur from the mental fatigue that accompanies a rigorous workload related to something enjoyable (Kaplan & Kaplan, 1982, p. 178). The student experience involves meeting expectations and deadlines while learning about new ideas and managing non-academic responsibilities. The authors consider James'

(1892) discussion on *voluntary* and *involuntary attention* in their research on the properties of stress and the construction of the restorative experience. They identify restorative qualities of nature with four specific properties comprised of *"being away, extent, fascination,* and *compatibility"* (Kaplan & Kaplan, 1982, p. 186). An escape from stress is part of feeling away and could apply to a mental or physical conception of removal. This leads to the second property extent, which relies on both connectedness and scope to provide the sense of a larger whole (Kaplan & Kaplan, 1982, p. 184).

Fascination is portrayed experiences that engage a person's attention without utilizing directed attention: a type of engagement with the environment that allows for interest or curiosity without mental taxation. Lastly, compatibility occurs when the effort required to complete a task is supported by the context (Kaplan & Kaplan, 1982, p. 186). They further discuss how a preferred environment is more likely to be restorative and that nature plays a powerful role in what is preferred; therefore, a natural environment will probably offer a restorative experience to a user. These locations are usually situated nearby and provide relief from everyday life. The authors believe deeper restorative experience has four levels that entail "clearing the head," recovering from mental fatigue, engaging in soft fascination, and allowing for reflection, an experience that involves introspective qualities related to a sense of self, life choices, and goals (Kaplan & Kaplan, 1982, p. 197).

Mapping and Affordance of Space

In the authors' view, people create cognitive maps, "schematic knowledge people have about a familiar environment," to move through spaces (Kaplan & Kaplan, 1982, p. 5). These maps can influence movement in locations frequented in daily life such as the university or college campus. The average community college student has likely created certain cognitive maps that support their movement throughout the campus where they attend class or visit resources such as the library, administrative offices, or athletic facilities. The campus attends to shared and solitary experiences because its design offers places for social engagement and others for quiet contemplation. Green landscapes present space to digest information, to reflect on concepts, and to relax in an environment that has restorative qualities.

Ulrich (1983) suggests that beyond preferences for certain visuals it is a widely held notion in urbanized countries that experiences with natural environments can be psychologically healthful (p. 113). He emphasizes the importance of considering contact with natural spaces in the planning and design of facilities and institutions where people are more likely to experience high levels of stress such as hospitals and schools. Likewise Tenneson and Cimprich investigate the relationship between attention and access to nature in a college environment. They posit students who have more natural views from their dormitory windows show higher levels of performance on measures of directed attention than those who have fewer natural views (Tennessen & Cimprich,1995, p. 78).

A supportive space is determined by the possiblities available to the user. Moreover, Gibson (1986) defines *affordances*, as "what the object offers the animal, what it provides or furnishes, either good or ill" (p. 127). He delineates between *positive* and *negative* affordances in terms of what one may be able to do with an object as opposed to how an object creates an obstacle or barrier. The ability to hide is also considered an affordance in an environment because concealment allows the user to go unnoticed within a space. Gibson states affordances "offer benefit or injury, life or death" (Gibson, 1986, p. 143). As a concept, it identifies the ability to sit, rest or retreat in a natural outdoor setting. In the author's view trees and grass add positive affordances whereas areas with excessively built environments create negative affordances, obstacles for the social or solitary experience outside.

Comparably, Appleton (1975) highlights *prospect* or *shelter*, places one can hide without being seen (p. 168). In the context of the campus environment, these concepts inform how design allows for solitary engagement with natural space in contrast to areas dedicated to group interaction. The interplay between solitary and social spaces may encourage both types of engagement in the campus environment. Campus design can attend to this reality with natural landscapes and green settings that allow for rejuvenation. In Kaplan and Kaplan's (1982) view, a lack of clarity in the spatial layout of an environment can in fact cause an individual to experience stress. In contrast when one is confronted with an environment that is logically structured, it communicates support and ease of functionality. Ultimately, in the absence of a clear spatial arrangement, the individual will experience feelings of confusion and distress.

Scholarly Identity

In *Design for Human Affairs* (1974), Deasy explores behavior at the Long Beach State University campus to appreciate the needs and experience of campus users. In this case, interviews revealed students wanted more places to study and eat comfortably outdoor as well as opportunities to meet casually with faculty outside classes or office hours. Observations revealed that students congregate around the entrance of buildings both before and after class (Deasy, 1974, p. 177). They also discovered students use areas outside of main buildings for socialization.

Characteristics of Space

In *Design for Human Affairs*, Deasy (1974) stresses students are eager to experience places on campus that can facilitate informal social interactions as well as solitary time around others in the outdoor spaces. Consequently, he proposes a redesign of campus entries to accommodate these specific needs by placing structures such as seating or steps at the entrance of main buildings for multiple purposes like meeting, talking, or eating (Deasy, 1974, p. 177). He also references the role of closeness or "getting together" as an important part of forming friendships. Many studies have documented the importance of proximity in the development of relationships at work or school, citing the closeness of their colleague's desk or cubical as a major factor in regular socialization. To that end, the authors reference another study on dormitories at the University of Chicago which states:

> In an analysis of friendship relationships . . . closeness or proximity was found to be precisely correlated to recognition and liking. Roommates were both recognized and liked more than floor mates, floor mates more than men in the same houses and housemates more than men in the same tower.
>
> (Deasy, 1974, p. 49)

The implications of this study on proximity and closeness could be profound in the context of integrating new students to the academic environment. Not to mention campus design can be instrumental in the ways that friendship and community are established.

Symbolic Qualities of the Campus

Dober's (1992) conversation in *Campus Design* assesses landmarks, which standardly include a chapel, library, administrative buildings, sports arena, and a quad (p. 18). These structures form a shared identity amongst a community of scholars. Similarly, Chapman addresses the monastic qualities of campus, a place where the built and natural environments are joined together, creating a feeling that stays with students long after they have left. He discusses how nature symbolizes openness, a departure from the colonial campus design typically cloistered and secluded. In the American academic landscape, there is a spatial connection to a larger setting beyond, one that is threaded through the campus itself (Chapman, 2006, p. 25).

Accordingly, Turner (1990) explains that the word *campus*, originating from the Latin meaning field, truly exemplifies the "unique physical character of the American college and university" (p. 4). The famous Frederick

Olmsted introduced the "cottage system" at the American university, which moved away from the monastic construction of buildings toward separate structures that formed a patchwork of academic units that were "park like," a design framework developed by the same man who produced New York's Central Park (Turner, 1990, p. 150). The underlying idea of this new system was reflected in the anti-elitist culture of the Land-Grant universities and the general sentiment of public higher education in the democratic Republic. The role of community in its expression of "the utopian social visions of the American imagination" is deployed through the construction and experience of the campus (Turner, 1990, p. 305). This is not representative of community colleges, where practical facilities cater to learning, administration, and athletics, without the tradition of structural landmarks found at the American university campus. A point further explored in the next chapter.

References

Appleton, J. (1975). *The experience of landscape.* New York, NY: John Wiley & Sons.

Bourdieu, P. (1984). *Distinction: A social critique of the judgement of taste.* London: Routledge & Kegan Paul.

Boyer, E. (1987). *College: The undergraduate experience in America.* New York, NY: Harper & Row Publishers.

Chapin, F. S. (1951). Some housing factors related to mental hygiene. Housing and mental hygiene. *The American Journal of Public Health, 41,* 839–845.

Chapman, P. (2006). *American places: In search of the twenty-first century campus.* Westport, CT: Praeger.

Cobban, A. B. (1988). *The Medieval English Universities: Oxford and Cambridge to c. 1500.* London. Routledge Press.

Community College Research Center. (2021). *Community college FAQs.* Retrieved from https://ccrc.tc.columbia.edu/Community-College-FAQs.html (accessed July 1, 2021).

Cooper-Marcus, C., & Wischemann, T. (1987, March–April). Outdoor places for living and learning. *Landscape Architecture,* 54–61.

Cooper-Marcus, C., & Wischemann, T. (1998). Campus Open Spaces. In Cooper-Marcus, C., & Francis, C. (Eds.), People Place: Design Guidelines for Urban Open Space. (2nd ed., pp. 175–206). John Wiley & Sons, Inc.

Deasy, C. M. & Laswell, T. E. (1985). *Designing places for people: A handbook on human behavior for architects, designers, and facility managers.* New York, NY: Watson-Guptill.

Deasy, C. M. (1974). *Design for human affairs.* New York, NY: Halsted Press.

Dober, R. (1992). *Campus design.* New York, NY: John Wiley & Sons.

Gibson, J. (1986). *The ecological approach to visual perception.* Hillsdale, NJ: Lawrence Erlbaum Associates Publishers.

Glazer, N., & Moynihan, D. (1970). *Beyond the melting pot: The Negroes, Puerto Ricans, Jews, Italians, and Irish of New York City.* Cambridge, MA: MIT Press.

Hall, E. (1969). *The hidden dimension: An anthropologist examines man's use of space in public and private.* New York, NY: Anchor Book.

Hiss, T. (1990). *The experience of place.* New York, NY: Vintage Books.

Jacobs, J. (1961). *The death and life of the great American cities.* New York, NY: Random House.

James, W. (1892). *Psychology: The briefer course.* New York, NY: Holt & Co.

Kaplan, S. (1995). The restorative benefits of nature: Toward an integrative framework. *The Journal of Environmental Psychology, 15,* 169–182.

Kaplan, S., & Kaplan, R. (1982). *Humanscape: Environments for people.* New York, NY: Praeger Publishers.

McFarland, A. L., Waliczek, T. M., & Zajicek, J. M. (2008). The relationship between student use of campus green spaces and perceptions of quality of life. *Horticology, 18*(2), 232–238.

Murphy, M., & Zirkel, S. (2015). Race and belonging in school: How anticipated and experienced belonging affect choice, persistence, and performance. *Teachers College, 117*(12), 1–40.

Naidoo, V. (2020). *Campus design and the community college experience: An exploration of stress, belonging and scholarly identity.* New York, NY: CUNY Academic Works.

Norberg-Schulz. C. (1979). *Genius loci. Towards a phenomenology of architecture.* New York, NY: Rizzoli International Publishers.

Saltrick, S. A. (1996). Campus of our own: Thoughts of a reluctant conservative. *Change, 28*(2), 58–62.

Speake, J., Edmondson, S., & Nawaz, H. (2013). Everyday encounters with nature: Students' perceptions and use of university campus green spaces. *Human Geographies, 7*(1), 21–31.

Tennessen, C. M., & Cimprich, B. (1995) Views to nature: Effects on attention. *Environmental Psychology, 15,* 77–85.

Turner, P. V. (1990). *Campus: An American planning tradition.* Cambridge, MA: The MIT Press.

Ulrich, R. (1983). Aesthetic and affective response to natural environment. In *Behavior and the natural environment.* New York, NY: Plenum Press.

Walton, G. M., & Cohen, G. L. (2007). A question of belonging: Race, social fit, and achievement. *Journal of Personality and Social Psychology, 92,* 82–96.

3 A Study on Bronx Community College
Rationale and Methodology

This chapter is primarily concerned with the relationship between campus design and student experience at Bronx Community College (BCC), part of the City University of New York (CUNY). To evaluate that, it was important to connect with the undergraduate student population and benefit from their engagement with the campus environment. The goal was to learn more about their habits and preferences. A mixed-methods approach provided detail on ways green space on campus had influenced their college experience, with reference to wellbeing, belonging, and scholarly identity. The study aimed to address how campus design, specifically green space, shapes the experience for a diverse student population at an urban community college. Participants discussed outdoor areas on campus, with an emphasis on green space in the quad and the seating that surrounds it. Campus landmarks referenced include The Hall of Fame for Great Americans, the front of the Library and North Hall Building, the outdoor seating area located in front of Meister Hall and Gould Hall Memorial Library. At this stage of the study, the intention was to collect information on student experience to contribute to a larger conversation on campus design, lived experience, and access to green space in the learning environment.

> The great obsession of the nineteenth century was, as we know, history: with its themes of development and of suspension, of crisis, and cycle, themes of the ever-accumulating past, with its great preponderance of dead men and the menacing glaciation of the world. The nineteenth century found its essential mythological resources in the second principle of thermodynamics. The present epoch will perhaps be above all the epoch of space. We are in the epoch of simultaneity: we are in the epoch of juxtaposition, the epoch of the near and far, of the side-by-side, of the dispersed. We are at a moment. I believe, when our experience of the world is less that of a long life developing through time than that of a network that connects points and intersects with its own skein.
> (Foucault & Miskowiec, 1986, p. 23)

DOI: 10.4324/9781003130598-3

From the Bible to Greek mythology, contact with green space has always suggested a sacred communion with nature. However, in the modern world, that relationship has changed. Urbanization has made these spaces less accessible and in turn more commodified. Today, green space signals prestige. Renowned landscape architect Frederick Law Olmsted, responsible for the iconic design found at New York's Central Park or countless campuses including Ivy League and Land-Grant colleges, stressed the presence of nature in the urban domain that could bring "rest and tranquility to the mind" (Olmsted, 1865/1968, p. 23). For that reason, community gardens and public parks make urban areas more desirable with the promise of solitude and nature. Green space is considered a luxury in the metropolis. Grass denotes a sense of tranquility needed for contemplation and reflection. In that way, exposure to nature can support the creation of new knowledge. Therefore, when students have access to green space in the learning environment, it is an investment in wellbeing. Users are encouraged to stay because the institution perceives contact with nature as beneficial. Turner (1990) states the campus represents the distinctive physical qualities of the American college, its integrity as a self-contained community and its architectural expression of educational and social ideals (p. 4). Perhaps there is a connection between academic trajectory and design. Many believe the standards of the institution are rooted in design as Dober (2000) asserts it is "the green environment that situates, serves, and symbolizes higher education" (p. xv).

Studies show that campus design and student perception are positively correlated to academics since students report higher levels of contentment, the result of exposure to nature on campus (McFarland et al., 2008, 2010; Sturner, 1972; Taylor et al., 2006; Lachowycz & Jones, 2014). In terms of wellbeing, exposure to natural settings contributes to lower levels of anxiety (Moore, 2021; Kaplan, 2001). Students from privileged backgrounds select their campus of choice based on beauty and sophistication as much as reputation, reinforcing the notion that institutions of higher education also offer a specific quality of life (Caws, 1970). Addressing wellbeing through campus design at the community college seems vital where 62 percent of full-time students and 73 percent of part-time students balance employment with school (AACC, 2021). The urban campus poses many challenges because the traditional concept of a learning environment must somehow be married with the dense grid design of the city landscape (Blaik, 2007). Calm must be achieved within chaos. Given the importance of the aesthetic qualities found in this landscape, the campus should offer an experience that encourages positive engagement with the built environment (Koenig, 2016).

With that in mind, three central questions were used to study the connection between lived and built environments. Chief among the different aspects of campus design investigated was location, specifically the urban landscape. New York City is famous for a whirlwind pace, reflected in its packed subways, competitive workforce, and expansive metropolitan area. This study focuses on the campus at Bronx Community College (BCC) because it has a unique traditional design situated in a complex urban framework. Research questions attend to the reality of the community college student experience at a commuter school.

Research Questions

How does campus design impact the student experience at a community college?
Does contact with green space on campus provide a restorative experience and relief from fatigue caused by directed attention?
Does campus design contribute to the development of a scholarly identity?

To further understand the role of green space at this campus the research design was constructed on a multi-phase exploration of student experience. For the purposes of this study, experience is defined by engagement with the physical space, a means of learning more about wellbeing, belonging, and scholarly identity. Creswell (2014) identifies the "strength of drawing on both qualitative and quantitative research and minimizing the limitations of both approaches" and thus a survey and focus group was used (p. 218). Research design must consider the most appropriate tools for data collection to properly address the questions a study sets out to answer. The use of multiple methods has been identified as valuable to the process of triangulation in that different methods can assess "one another seeing if methods with different strengths and limitations all support the same conclusion" (Maxwell, 2013, p. 102). Further, Greene (2007) refers to the merits of multiple tools of assessment for *complementarity and expansion* or the ability to examine an experience from various perspectives (pp. 101–104). The author emphasizes the importance of the mixed-methods approach because of what he refers to as divergent perspectives that emerge from different approaches of information gathering (Greene, 2007, pp. 79–83).

Stage One (Survey)

First, IRB approval was attained for this study, which used human research subjects. A sample group of two hundred students was selected using the campus listserv. With the survey method, Lincoln and Guba (1985) recall "naturalistic inquiry relies upon purposeful rather than representative sampling" (p. 102). The Office of Academic Affairs assisted with access to students, sending an email invitation to complete the survey. Recipients included those who met specific criteria:

- At least 18 years of age and over
- Enrolled in credit-bearing courses in Fall 2019

At the end of the survey, students were given the option to volunteer for a focus group on campus design. A one-page questionnaire was developed to collect data on student experience of campus design at BCC. The survey method made it possible to reach a large segment of the student population on campus and was accessible on multiple digital formats which enhanced student participation. Being able to access the survey on a smartphone or computer was essential in terms of completion rate because the average commuter student has little free time and travels throughout the city. In this study, the survey had two functions in that it reached many students and provided more general feedback on student experience of campus design. Participants were incentivized to complete the survey with the chance to win 1 of 63 Amazon gift cards worth $10 each. An administrator at BCC shared the survey invitation multiple times on the campus listserv between September and November of 2019. The survey was divided into four sections to identify demographic information (age, race, and gender), use and perceptions of green spaces, wellbeing, and scholarly identity as stated in Appendix A.

The survey contained a combination of closed and open-ended questions. Closed-ended questions were useful for determining basic information where a dichotomous structure was appropriate. One positive aspect of this type of question is that it allows students to select a response with minimal ambiguity, potentially found in other question types. Another point is that participants can swiftly select their response because choices are limited. In a survey with over 30 questions that require a commuter student to reflect on experiential aspects of design, brevity and timing were important. This line of inquiry supported open-ended responses that participants required to provide specific details about locations and preferences on campus. Here the process of reflection was integral because students were asked to consider engagement with green space, adding a rich collection of responses that highlighted preferred locations. On the other hand, the absence of predetermined responses, various modalities used to complete the survey (phones, tablets, or computers) and potential time constraints (being busy and/or tired) produced some less useful feedback that was either illegible or irrelevant. Overall, this combination of closed and open-ended questions was used both carefully and sparingly in consideration of the advantages and limitations listed earlier. The majority of the survey used a scaled question format that proved helpful for a number of reasons. First, the responses offered a range of feelings toward spaces and places on campus. Participants could assess how frequency and preference overlap. Second, the scaled responses gave choices that could be selected both easily and quickly using any modality (phone or computer). Third, a sparing interplay between closed and open-ended questions organically built on the assessment of experience based on degree. In this way, the survey encouraged students to consider their feelings by substantiating them with examples, preferences, and habitual activity. As a researcher, this was very informative about student experience because the scaled responses produced valuable graphic representations that were complemented by the open-ended and closed-ended format.

The purpose of this survey was to give students an opportunity to define and explain their experiences on campus. It was used in conjunction with the qualitative data for a deeper understanding of their time on campus. Once the surveys were completed, descriptive statistics were used to understand how variables such as gender, race, and age compare in frequency to questions regarding student experience. Qualitative data from the open-ended questions was coded to assist in making the Likert-type scale more robust.

Survey Design and Campus Design

The survey asked students to reflect on their engagement with nature on campus through questions regarding their emotions and the physical environment. This line of inquiry was inspired by McFarland et al.'s (2008) study which examined how "undergraduate student use of campus green spaces and perceptions of quality of life were related to each other" (p. 232). This study explores the social aspects of contact with green space and how that contributes to an overall feeling of wellness and sociability in students. Many participants recall brief encounters with nature when walking to class or doing physical activities with friends, examples of engagement with green space that decreased the typical stresses that characterize student life on campus.

Definitions of Natural Space

In *The Experience of Nature: A Psychological Perspective*, Kaplan and Kaplan (1989) highlight nature can be very broadly defined to adapt to various settings where both green and living areas exist:

> ...nature here is not limited to those faraway, vast and pristine places where there has been limited human intervention, or those places designated as 'natural areas' by some governmental authority.

> ...We are referring to those places near and far, common and unusual, managed and unkempt, big, small, and in-between, where plants grow by human design or even despite it.
> Nature includes parks, meadows, open spaces and abandoned fields, trees, and backyard gardens.
> We are referring to areas that would often be described as green... Nature includes plants and various forms of vegetation... also includes landscapes or places with plants.
>
> (p. 2)

This study approached the concept of green space with an appreciation for Kaplan and Kaplan's work, attempting to address the often-abstract meanings assigned to this term. Together the survey and focus group offered students an idea of what constitutes natural settings on campus.

Acknowledging this study explores the relationship between campus design, namely green space, and the student experience of wellbeing, belonging, and scholarly identity, the following studies informed this research in various ways and supported its methodological process.

Wellbeing in the Survey Design

According to McFarland et al. (2008), "researchers have found that students' perception of their overall academic experience and the campus environment is related to academic accomplishment" (p. 232). In their study of the relationship between undergraduate students use of campus green spaces and perceptions of quality of life, they used an online survey to assess experience (McFarland et al., 2008). Collecting demographic information, they identified characteristics such as academic standing, gender, and ethnicity in addition to employing frequency statistics to delineate between high or low users of campus green space. Statements that assessed engagement with green spaces on campus and general quality of life were used for comparison. The survey questions were divided into discreet sections, namely green space usage (high and low usage), affective domain ("I feel restless" or "I find it easy to get to know people") and demographic information (male, female, or non-binary) (McFarland et al., 2008). Their categories served as a foundation for the study at BCC because they support the exploration of engagement with space and the social-emotional dimensions of student experience referring to demographic information on age, gender, and race. Relatedly, their concept of high and low use of campus green space was also implemented to identify the type of activities students engage in when on campus. The Likert scale encouraged participants to reflect on the rate of usage, asking them to assess the frequency with which they used campus green space.

Lastly, Attention Restoration Theory (ART) is visited in both the survey and focus group discussion to better understand the healing capacity of green space on campus, distinguishing them from other environments associated with stressors that involve prolonged periods of concentration.

Belonging in the Survey Design

In "Campus and Outdoor Spaces," Cooper-Marcus and Wischemann (1998) consider how the physical environment influences experience using behavior trace analysis, activity mapping, and formal interviews. In the study at Berkeley University, behavior trace analysis encouraged students to reflect on their experience of campus design. Similarly at BCC, the trace analysis method helped students recall time spent in campus green space. This commentary was further probed in the focus group discussion held on campus. Moreover, it was imperative to understand social interaction facilitated by campus design. Students were asked to consider different types of activities they engaged in while on campus including social or solitary events such as eating, sunbathing, and people watching. Questions focused on language proposed by Cooper-Marcus and Wischemann (1998), namely the front yard and back yard concepts that view the spatial design of the campus from an intimate perspective. Terms that frame the college as more of an abode than a school like the home base, a place on campus that users are inclined to return to because of its experiential qualities. In these spaces, users feel relaxed, safe, and at home. Belonging is understood through engagement with design that considers the concept of the learning campus, featured in the survey, and focus group with targeted questions related to habitual activity. Kenney et al. (2005) describe the learning campus as a place that "maximizes the probability of chance encounters and encourages lingering ... whether by chance or by plan ... an exciting place where students and faculty alike enjoy 'hanging out,' whether alone or in groups" (p. 39).

Scholarly Identity in the Survey Design

Additionally, students were asked about social belonging using questions about interactions with friends, classmates, and faculty on campus. These relationships were assessed in the context of understanding engagement with campus design as it relates to social dimensions, more specifically how those relationships shaped their perception of being a student. Studies have shown that social belonging is influenced by moments of acknowledgment within the academic environment, positive interactions with teachers and classmates that serve a motivating function. Students that feel they are part of the social fabric are more inclined to channel that sense of belonging into their performance (Dweck et al., 2014). Since the Education Reform movement, there has been a long-standing debate on the connection between learning experience and learning environment in the United States. Critical to the discussion is a further study on prosocial behaviors fostered by aesthetic choices and social interaction (Moore & Lackney, 1994). Understanding the development of scholarly identity within the context of the academic environment is necessary. This is primarily because of deficits observed in prison facilities and hospitals where rehabilitation can be hindered by design choices that overlook the necessity of natural light or stimulating visuals. In each instance, performance and perception are interrelated.

Stage Two (Focus Group)

In stage two, ten students were invited to participate in a focus group. Both groups met on the same day with discussion sessions held in the morning and in the afternoon. Participants were compensated for their time with a $30 Amazon gift card, which they received at the end of the focus group. The purpose of stage two was to learn more about how campus design has impacted their overall college experience. A one-time session was held over a 45-minute period where students engaged in a walking tour of the campus to indicate areas they referenced during the discussion. The conversation was audio-recorded and analyzed to identify notable themes related to the experience of campus design. Given the format of the meeting was a group conversation, this stage relied mainly on open-ended questions except for a few closed-ended. Each group was limited to five participants which proved beneficial because every student was able to share feedback, adding an inclusive aspect to the conversation. Some drawbacks of the small group were excessive or unrelated responses likely connected to being outside of a formal setting such as a classroom where relevance and social ques are more obvious. In this way, students were inclined to elaborate on responses given by other participants. This posed an interesting challenge because on one hand it lessened the degree of originality in comments, yet it also lowered inhibition. Students were more likely to respond because other participants had already established a response they could develop further. Notable observations on this method include reuse of language, limited ideas presented, and increased potential for consensus in feedback instead of ideas that directly contradict the status quo. Conversely, the open-ended format certainly cut the initial tension that exists in a social gathering where everyone is new. With each response, students were able to relate experiences to each other in a very meaningful way because participants observed similarities that were often deemed part of ritualistic behavior that constitutes traditions.

Campus Design in the Focus Group

This research considers previous scholarship on campus design and attempts to identify positive design choices at BCC that could potentially assist other campuses to reimagine green space. Placemaking, an approach that allows for public space to be repurposed is one way to address space constraints in the physical environment. Tennessen and Cimprich (1995) suggest "if natural views from windows do have positive effects on student capacity to direct attention, this would have considerable implications for the placement and design of dormitories". Natural views are therefore related to performance because "students require strong attention to successfully master the multiple demands of education in the university setting" (Grayson, 1985). Likewise, Speake et al. (2013) believe, "people and green spaces are tied by interconnectivities which can be premised in affective and emotional responses and ultimately reflected in people's perceptions of their environment and their articulation of them." Finally, Abu-Ghazzeh (1999) and McFarland et al. (2008) assess the implications of campus green space "noting that perception of a place or place meaning can comprise three types of knowledge, about the place, its affective quality, and behavior that occurs there," implying further research is needed. The focus group was intentionally staged as a walking tour of the BCC campus to place built and lived environment in direct conversation with one another. Students narrated their perception of these spaces, speaking to their personal experiences with the campus design namely the ways it had shaped the social and academic dimensions of their student life. The walking tour was inspired by Edward T. Hall's discussion of proxemics (Hall, 1966; Hall and Hall, 1990).

Wellbeing in the Focus Group

Given the role of stress in the college experience, wellbeing was a central focus of this study. That initial shift from high school leaves post-secondary students particularly vulnerable to the feeling of overstimulation and burnout. Students must adapt to a new set of expectations for academic and social performance. Those who succeed, acclimate quickly to the new environment. This is likely because they cultivate a strong work ethic and recognize social connectedness facilitates integration in the new context. To that end, in the eighties and nineties scholarship emerged on the process of attention-restoring experience, highlighted by Kaplan's (1995) studies on the experiential aspects of natural environments. Furthermore, Hall's study of proxemics emphasized the relationship between lived experience and spatial environment, highlighting, "no matter what happens in the world of human beings, it happens in a spatial setting, and the design of that setting has a deep and persisting influence on the people in that setting" (Hall and Hall, 1990, p. xi). Drawing on Ulrich's research (1979), on the relationship between wellbeing and natural views, the walking tour encouraged participants to reflect on the juxtaposition of urban and campus landscapes as it relates to lived experience. His research relied on a comparative analysis that highlighted the effects of urban and natural views, a focus brought to this study at BCC, in a discourse on space.

Belonging in the Focus Group

Cooper-Marcus and Wischemann's (1998) research at the UC Berkeley campus employed the terms front porch and home turf to spatially orient students within the campus environment emphasizing experiential aspects of the space. Participants were able to share ways the built and natural environment on campus had contributed to their sense of belonging. These concepts were explored in both the survey and focus group at BCC because descriptive language offers deeper understanding of lived experience. These terms connote a sense of community reminding the user of the intimate qualities of the outdoor home environment. In this way, it was possible to learn whether students experience these spaces in a personal way, like a second home. The informality of the focus group method, a small gathering defined by cohesion and belonging, eased the process of information sharing during the walking tour (Peters, 1993; Vaughn et al., 1996).

Scholarly Identity in the Focus Group

In view of Deasy and Lasswell's (1985) study of social behavior in campus spaces at Berkeley, survey analysis at BCC encouraged participants to specify preferred locations on campus, while also making the distinction between time spent on work versus leisure. Similarly, interview methods in the focus group at BCC asked participants to describe areas on campus that could enhance the academic and social dimensions of their student experience with classmates or faculty in outdoor spaces. Questions required participants to define their habits and interactions in terms of academic identity. Together, they were able to articulate feelings while hearing other participant reflections that contrasted with their own experience. In this way, the focus group at BCC was situated in the idea that physical environment reflects the attitudes and values of the institution. Sturner (1972) proposes "man projects himself onto his environment"; therefore, student narratives were used to learn how space can support the development of student identity.

A Brief History of CUNY

The City University of New York can trace its origins back to the nineteenth century about 20 years before the introduction of the Land-Grant Act, yet it would experience its most rapid period of expansion in the mid-twentieth century. The story of the institution began when Townsend Harris, a successful businessman, had a vision of a Free Academy, a revolutionary concept, as "a municipal college was something unheard of" at that time though state colleges and universities had already been in existence (Traub, 1994, p. 22). In *City on a Hill* (1994), Traub describes the establishment of the *Free Academy* in 1847 as "the radical and controversial social experiment" imagined by Harris as a public academy of higher learning that would "educate the whole people" (p. 21). Known as the "Harvard of the proletariat," it was often referred to as "City on a hill."

Fabricant and Brier (2016) recall the creation of Hunter College two decades later in 1870, a Normal school where women prepared to be teachers (p. 51). This academy of higher education eventually grew to include a branch campus in the Bronx, currently known as Lehman College. In *CUNY's First Fifty Years: Triumphs and Ordeals of a People's University* (2018) Picciano and Jordan explain soon after City and Hunter College were introduced, in 1910 Brooklyn and Queens became sights for evening classes that provided access to higher education to the residents of the outer boroughs (p. 13). The growing demand for classes combined with the exceptional distance between the Manhattan campuses and the student body commuting from one borough to another, warranted the creation of additional CUNY campuses. This led to the introduction of Brooklyn College in 1930, which the authors describe as the first publicly funded co-educational school in New York City, followed by Queens College in 1937 (Picciano & Jordan, 2018, pp. 14–16).

Levine (1986) emphasizes that between 1920 and 1930 enrollment at City College had increased by 353 percent, with additional growth of 228 percent by 1940. In total, The College of the City of New York (CCNY) went from roughly 3,000 students in 1920 to 24,000 in the span of two decades (Levine, 1986, p. 85). In the postwar expansion period, higher education experienced a boom in terms of development, which culminated in the creation of several new campuses at CUNY. Rudy (1949) states that "CUNY's growth was an educational evolution as opposed to a revolution" because its expansion was a rational response to New York City's own development (p. 397). These new additions varied in structure to attend to the rapid increase in the student population in New York. Two- and four-year colleges were established in the Bronx, Brooklyn, Queens, and Staten Island. The initial expansion of community colleges began with Staten Island, which opened in 1956, Bronx in 1957 and Queensborough in 1959 (Picciano &

Jordan, 2018, pp. 18–19). Rudy (1949) asserts in the period between 1920 and 1930, City College students "came largely from lower income groups and had grown up in homes where there had been continuous and severe struggle for existence" (p. 398). According to Levine (1986), in its early days, the City College offered "a way out of the working class into teaching or other white-collar professions" (p. 87). Today CUNY is composed of 25 campuses that define the third-largest public institution in the country. More recent additions include graduate and professional education that uphold the mission of the City University of New York (CUNY, 2022).

New York and Higher Education

In *The College of the City of New York: A History 1847–1947*, Rudy explains how the urban landscape evolved between the early nineteenth and twentieth century with the transformation of residential neighborhoods into places of business (p. 382). It was at this time the city responded to the growing numbers of high school graduates by relocating City College to Washington Heights in 1907. The vastness of the city and the limited transportation available restricted students from attending City or Hunter College in Manhattan. This inspired Brooklyn, which was the largest growing borough, to advocate for its own satellite of CCNY, eventually established in 1917. The initial classes were conducted at night and were extended to Queens, though the demand for more permanent sites located in the outer boroughs became so great that it led to the creation of Brooklyn College and later Queens College (p. 389).

That same strength of community would return to the Bronx during the fifties, where local groups advocated for a campus that could cater to the higher education needs of borough residents. New York City and its outer boroughs would define public education with a comprehensive system of colleges comprised of senior and junior schools. Postwar policies and social movements would shift the image of the traditional wealthy college student by introducing a new type of learner who came from more humble beginnings. These students commuted to school, came from working-class homes and would eventually achieve upward social mobility. In turn, campus design would also adjust to accommodate the distinct social change taking place in America.

Rationale for Study

With this scholarship on green space in mind, the urban environment has evolved in ways that impact learning for all. The research conducted at BCC is situated in this dialogue on green space, because it explores the relationship between campus design and student experience, specifically wellbeing, belonging, and scholarly identity. This study posits that reflection is a necessary consideration in campus design because it is tied to informal social interactions supporting wellbeing, belonging and scholarly identity. Engaging in the process of information sharing on campus supports the feeling of belonging, which can develop a sense of wellbeing and successful academic performance. This can be accomplished with positive social interactions and regular exposure to natural settings. Peterkin's (2013) research on student experience investigates on-campus housing. Time spent on campus shapes the college experience in many ways. This seemingly insignificant engagement with campus space can have a long-lasting impact because, as Peterkin (2013) explains, "it forms a community of scholars that will live together and learn together and become colleagues for life." Morever, his study suggests that the rate of engagement with green space on campus can encourage positive social interactions. It proposes that students, who are regular users of green spaces on campus, experience a higher quality of life, which fosters the process of information sharing with other students and increases the potential for reflection, the cornerstone of wellbeing.

This aligns with McFarland et al.'s (2008) findings that revealed, "in general, students who used the campus green spaces more frequently perceived their quality of life as higher when compared with those students who used green spaces less frequently" (p. 234). Scholarship explored in this chapter considered research on campus design that influenced this study of green space at BCC. There is an immediacy associated with this type of research as CUNYs community colleges are where New York's historically underserved communities converge in the pursuit of public higher education. Exploring the relationship between location and the creation of new knowledge can inform our understanding of effective choices in campus design that support learning.

References

Abu-Ghazzeh, T. M. (1999). Communicating behavioral research to campus design: Factors affecting the perception and use of outdoor spaces at the University of Jordan. *Environment and Behavior, 31*(6), 764–804.

American Association of Community Colleges. (2021). *Fast facts*. Retrieved from www.aacc.nche.edu/wp-content/uploads/2021/03/AACC_2021_FastFacts.pdf (accessed May 5, 2021).

Blaik, O. (2007). Campuses in cities: Places between engagement and retreat. *The Chronicle of Higher Education, 53*(25), 25.

Caws, P. (1970). Design for a university. *Daedalus, 99*, 84–107.

Cooper-Marcus, C., & Wischemann, T. (1998). Campus outdoor spaces. In C. C. Marcus & C. Francis (Eds.), *People places: Design guidelines for urban open space*. New York, NY: John Wiley & Sons.

Creswell, J. W. (2014). *Research design: Qualitative, quantitative, and mixed methods approaches*. Thousand Oaks, CA: SAGE Publications.

City University of New York. (2022). Mission Statement. *About CUNY*. Retrieved from: https://www.cuny.edu/about/. Accessed on March 25, 2022.

Deasy, C. M. & Lasswell, T. E. (1985). *Designing places for people: A handbook on human behavior for architects, designers, and facility managers*. New York, NY: Watson-Guptill.

Dober, R. (2000). *Campus landscape: Function, forms, features*. New York, NY: John Wiley & Sons.

Dweck, C., Walton, G. M., & Cohen, G. L. (2014). *Academic tenacity: Mindsets and skills that promote long-term learning*. Seattle, WA: Bill and Melinda Gates Foundation.

Fabricant, M., & Brier, S. (2016). *Austerity blues: Fighting for the soul of public higher education*. Baltimore, MD: Johns Hopkins University Press.

Foucault, M., & Miskowiec, J. (1986). Of other spaces. *Diacritics, 16*(1), 22–27.

Grayson, P. A. (1985). College time: Implications for student mental health services. *Journal of American College Health, 33*(5), 198–204.

Greene, J. C. (2007). *Mixed methods in social inquiry*. San Francisco, CA: Jossey-Bass.

Hall, E. (1966). *The hidden dimension: An anthropologist examines man's use of space in public and private*. New York, NY: Anchor Book.

Hall, E. T., & Hall, M. R. (1990). *Understanding cultural differences*. Yarmouth, ME: Intercultural Press.

Kaplan, R. (2001). The nature of the view from home: Psychological benefits. *Environment and Behavior, 33*(4), 507–542.

Kaplan, R., & Kaplan, S. (1989). *The experience of nature*. Cambridge, MA: Cambridge University Press.

Kaplan, S. (1995). The restorative benefits of nature: Toward an integrative framework. *The Journal of Environmental Psychology, 15*, 169–182.

Kenney, D. R., Dumont, R., & Kenney, G. (2005). *Mission and place: Strengthening learning and community through campus design*. Westport. CT: Praeger Publishing.

Koenig, C. (2016). How architects can help community colleges promote community on campus. *Building Design & Construction*. Retrieved from www.bdcnetwork.com/blog/how-architects-can-help-community-colleges-promote-community-campus (accessed January 20, 2020).

Lachowycz, K., & Jones, A. (2014). Does walking explain associations between access to greenspace and lower mortality? *Social Science & Medicine (1982), 107*(100), 9–17.

Levine, D. O. (1986). *The American college and the culture of aspiration, 1915–1940*. Ithaca, NY: Cornell University.

Lincoln, Y., & Guba, E. (1985). *The naturalistic inquiry*. London: SAGE.

Maxwell, J. (2013). *Qualitative research design: An interactive approach*. Thousand Oaks, CA: SAGE.

McFarland, A. L., Waliczek, T. M., & Zajicek, J. M. (2008) The relationship between student use of campus green spaces and perceptions of quality of life. *Horticology, 18*(2), 232–238.

McFarland, A. L., Waliczek, T. M., & Zajicek, J. M. (2010). Graduate student use of campus green spaces and the impact on their perceptions of quality of life. *HortTechnology*, 186–192.

Moore, G., & Lackney, J. (1994). Educational facilities for the twenty-first century: Research Analysis and design patterns. *Center for Architecture and Urban Planning Research Books, 32*.

Moore, J. (2021). *Mentally restorative areas for students: Impacts of nature on psychophysiological state*. Honors Thesis. University of Tennessee at Chattanooga. Chattanooga, TN.

Olmsted, F. L. (1968). The value and care of parks. In R. Nash (Ed.), *The American environment: Readings in the history of conservation* (pp. 18–24). Reading, MA: Addison-Wesley. (Original work published 1865)

Peterkin, C. (2013). Colleges design new housing as an experience to engage and retain students. *The Chronicle of Higher Education*. Retrieved from www.chronicle.com/article/Colleges-Design-New-Housing-as/136713/ (accessed December 14, 2017).

Peters, D. A. (1993). Improving quality requires consumer input: Using focus groups. *Journal of Nursing Care Quality, 7*, 34–41.

Picciano, A. G., & Jordan, C. R. (2018). *CUNY's first fifty years: Triumphs and ordeals of a people's university*. New York, NY: Routledge.

Rudy, W. S. (1949). *The college of the City of New York*. New York, NY: City College Press.

Speake, J., Edmondson, S., & Nawaz, H. (2013). Everyday encounters with nature: Students' perceptions and use of university campus green spaces. *Human Geographies, 7*(1), 21–31.

Sturner, W. F. (1972). Environmental code: Creating a sense of place on the college campus. *The Journal of Higher Education, 43*, 97–109.

Taylor, A., & Kuo, M. (2006). Is contact with nature important for healthy child development? State of the evidence. *Children and their Environments: Learning, Using and Designing Spaces*, 124–140.

Tennessen, C. M., & Cimprich, B. (1995). Views to nature: Effects on attention. *Environmental Psychology, 15*, 77–85.

Traub, J. (1994). *City on a hill: Testing the American dream at city college*. New York, NY: Addison-Wesley Publishing.

Turner, P. V. (1990). *Campus: An American planning tradition*. Cambridge, MA: The MIT Press.

Ulrich, R. (1979). Visual Landscapes and Psychological Well-Being. Landscape Research-LANDSC RES. 4. 17–23. 10.1080/01426397908705892.

Vaughn, S., Schumm, J. S., & Sinagub, J. (1996). *Focus group interviews in education and psychology*. Thousand Oaks, CA: SAGE.

4 Student Perception, Use, and Wellbeing on Campus

This chapter examines findings on student experience of green space in terms of wellbeing, belonging, and scholarly identity. Student experience is assessed using engagement with the physical environment, specifically green space. At a community college, academics are often balanced with employment and family responsibilities that influence the way space is used and the amount of time spent on campus. These two aspects of experience inform student perception of wellbeing. Social networks often emerge from study groups, office hours, or campus events; thus, academic and social interactions can contribute to the development of scholarly identity. These interactions nurture a sense of belonging in the physical environment, one that is reflected by use. That sense of belonging is further cultivated with time spent on campus and in locations where students go to socialize or to be alone. When green spaces are inviting, there is a desire to return to them.

These same qualities found in the academic environment support restorative experience. Pathways and benches strategically placed throughout the campus function as social cues for engagement with these outdoor spaces. To that end, tucked away in the historic University Heights neighborhood of the Bronx, the traditional campus design of BCC feels like something of an oasis from the rest of the world. This chapter will offer insight on the experience of its campus design with survey data and thematically organized narratives.

Survey Analysis

A survey was used to understand student experience of campus design. In the fall of 2019, students who were over the age of 18 and enrolled in credit-bearing courses were emailed an invitation to complete a survey online. Approximately, 6,410 students received the invitation from the campus listserv and 156 completed the survey. As is often the case with research on student experience, the results were not generalizable or a representative sample size, though the demographic information did correspond with institutional data on BCC (BCC, 2018a).

Profile of the Survey Participants

Demographic information represented an age range from 18 to 54, the largest group being 19- and 20-year-olds. Participants were asked to identify gender from three categories including male, female, and non-binary. Approximately, 65 percent identified as female with 34 percent male and 1 percent non-binary, consistent with The American Association of Community Colleges report which states 57 percent of students at community college are female and less than 22 years of age (AACC, 2021).

Most participants were Liberal Arts and Science majors at 56 percent, or Criminal Justice at 17 percent. Traditionally, Liberal Arts and Science majors largely contribute to the high transfer rate at BCC as 46 percent of students eventually attend four-year colleges within or beyond the CUNY system. (BCC, 2018a). Figure 4.1 indicates the racial composition of participants, with 66 percent identifying as Hispanic (of any race) and 21 percent Black or African American. Accordingly, BCC serves a very diverse student population. One quite different from their NYU counterparts of the

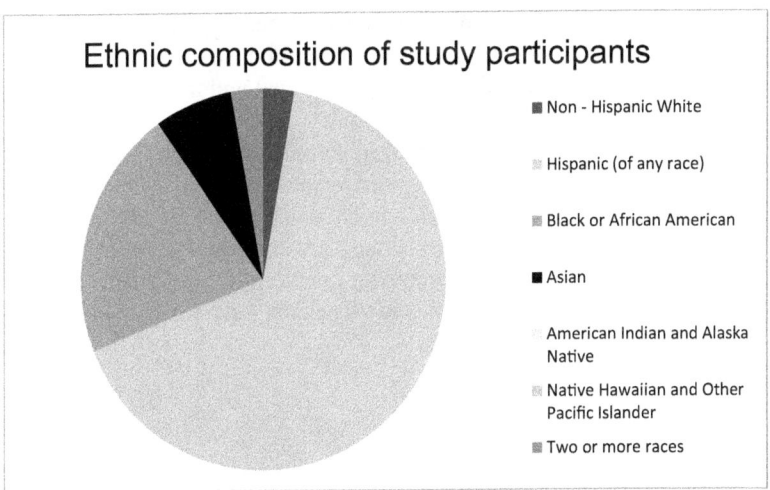

Figure 4.1 Race

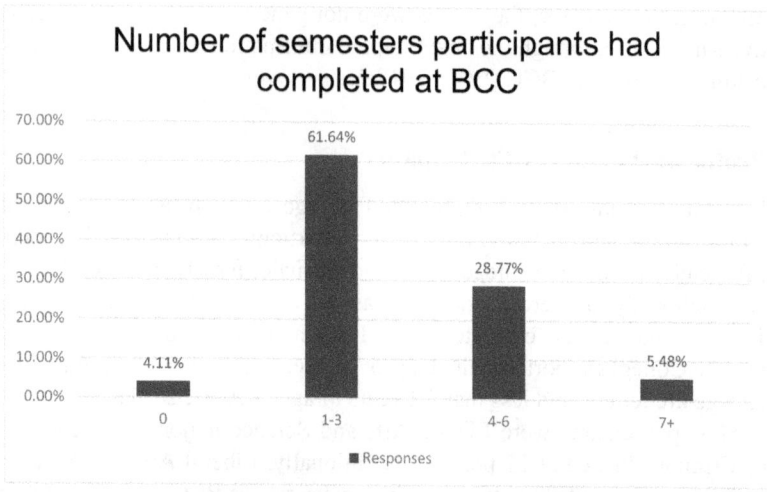

Figure 4.2 Semesters Completed at BCC

past, since student demographics of today have shifted to mirror communities that currently live in the Bronx and are affected by challenging social factors related to race, age and social class. In 2018, institutional data indicated Hispanic-identifying students totaled 61 percent whereas 33 percent identified as Black/African American. Once again, survey results reflected demographic information that supported national and institutional data on community colleges.

Figure 4.2 shows the total amount of completed semesters at BCC with 62 percent having completed one to three semesters, followed by 29 percent with four to six. BCC states that 20 percent of their students graduate within three years, as well as 46 percent transfer within the CUNY system and graduate in four. These are encouraging outcomes when 51 percent of the student population are employed, and 40 percent have a household income of less than $15,000 (BCC, 2018a).

Time Outside

Students were asked to assess contact with green space on campus. The first question focused on time spent at BCC. A six-point Likert scale was used with a range of responses: never, rarely, sometimes, pretty often, regularly,

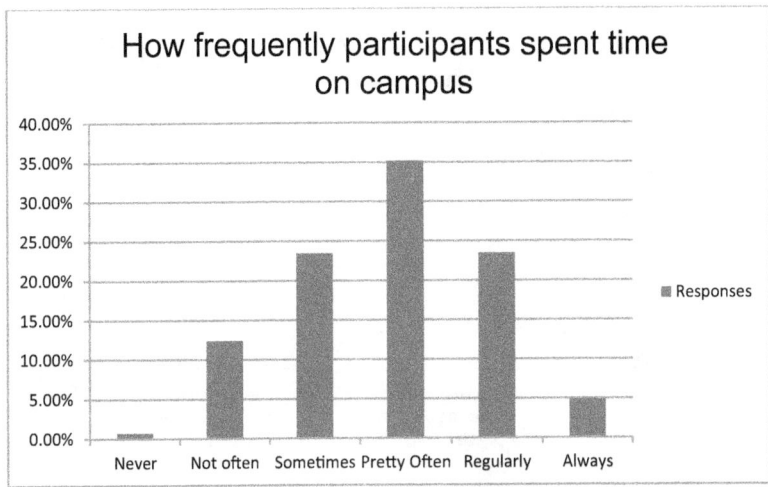

Figure 4.3 Time Spent on Campus

and always. Figure 4.3 indicates students generally do spend time on campus. More specifically, 58 percent of users selected either "pretty often" or "regularly" in reference to being on campus. Despite the considerable time constraints and inner-city travel involved in a commuter student's schedule participant responses suggest spending time on campus is a priority. To that end, roughly half of respondents reported they spend time with friends in green space while on campus further substantiated by the 68 percent who stated a positive range of response about general time spent in green space.

Survey data constructs an image of a student who can often be found with friends in outside areas on campus that are near green spaces. Further in their everyday lives, students clearly enjoy spending time in gardens or parks Acknowledging the importance participants placed on contact with natural settings, inside and outside of campus, highlights ways students value time spent in green space.

Comfort

Time spent on campus can offer insight on experiential aspects of design, such as feeling welcome or at ease. Comfort was evaluated using a Likert scale that consisted of: not at all comfortable, not very comfortable,

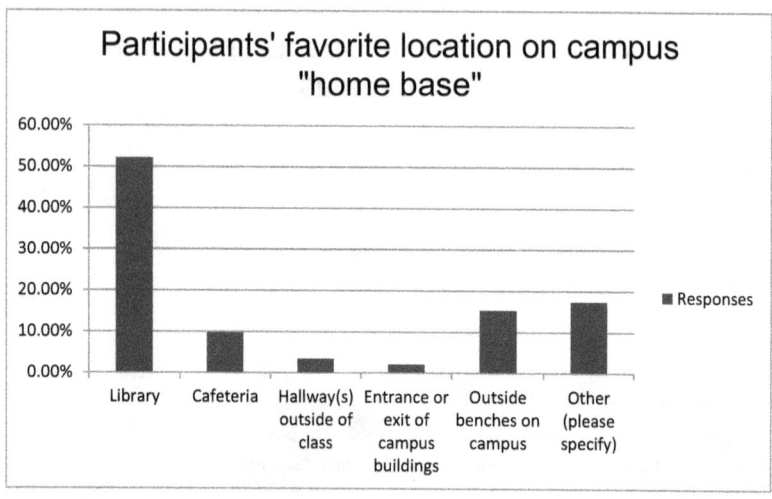

Figure 4.4 Locations Visited on Campus Regularly

somewhat comfortable, pretty comfortable, very comfortable, and completely comfortable. A total of 78 percent of participants selected positive responses in the range of "pretty comfortable" to "completely comfortable" with no one identifying themselves as being totally uncomfortable. At BCC, over half the student population are the first in their family to go to college and are employed with 72 percent dependent on financial aid, meaning success in post-secondary education requires determination (BCC, 2018a). This aligns with the national average which states that 29 percent of community college students are the first generation in their household to attend college with 62 percent that work in addition to attending school full time (AACC, 2021). Figure 4.4 represents locations on campus participants visit regularly. For approximately half of respondents that place was the North Hall and Library building, second to the Hall of Fame for Great Americans or benches located in outside areas on campus. Similarly, when students were asked to describe their comfort level in these spaces, responses ranged from "pretty comfortable" to "completely comfortable."

Students expressed pride for the Northeast side of the campus, where new and traditional design choices are reflected in the architecture. They describe feeling at home in the North Hall and Library building which indicates a positive relationship to structural modernity and academic tradition reflected in the aesthetic of this section of the campus. In this building, private study rooms allow students to work independently or in groups. The North Hall and Library building stands at a central point on campus between the cafeteria and Gould Memorial Hall, an official heritage site. Located at the boundary of the College, The Hall of Fame highlights contributions of great Americans. Known for its intimate quality, it encourages contemplation. In this space, it is possible to engage in soft fascination through contact with natural views and relieve the fatigue derived from directed attention required in class. The tranquility found here is like that of a library, since both spaces are conducive to solitary reflection or small gatherings. Important aspects of campus design for community college students who are building a scholarly identity through a sense of belonging and wellbeing.

Social Interaction

More than half of survey respondents said they socialize with friends on campus. Therefore, having a designated group on campus can influence feelings about college. Group members share information, offer comfort, and help build community. From the Ivy league to the state school system, social networks are the cornerstone of the university experience. Arguably, these networks are even more essential to success at community college given the potential for additional responsibility at home and work.

In contrast, other participants said they do not often talk to faculty on campus, and usually spend time alone. Behavior that seems typical of a community college student more focused on degree completion, perhaps using the campus in restorative ways that involves less engagement with those around them. In this way, living on campus can support the social aspects of student life.

Wellbeing

Relatedly, Figure 4.5 indicates participants feel stressed about college in general though they expressed feeling less stressed when they are on campus. Moderate to increased levels of stress described could be attributed to daily life, the result of expectations associated with college as opposed to contact with its built and lived environment. Still, it is necessary to learn more about how aesthetic shapes learning. Specifically, to increase knowledge on the benefits of modern versus traditional design choices and student preference as it relates to comfort and wellbeing.

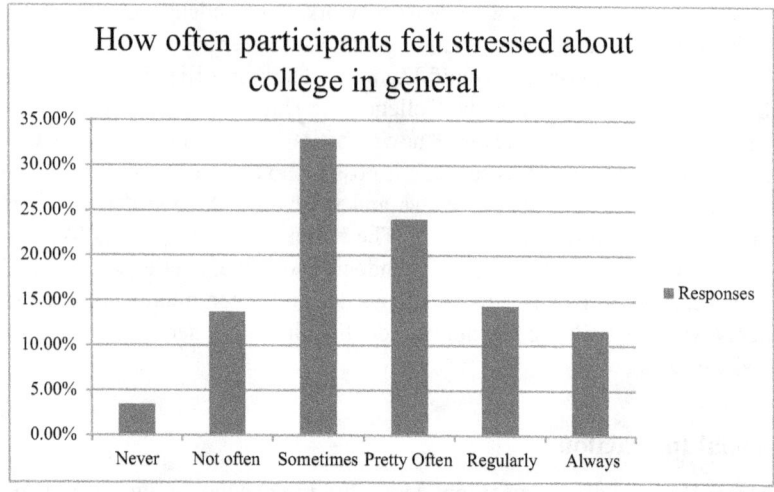

Figure 4.5 Stressed about College in General

Scholarly Identity

Most participants said the experience of being a student felt comfortable. Additionally, approximately 76 percent shared they think about course content when they are on campus. Yet despite their perceived comfort at college, regular discussions with faculty are uncommon for them. Time constraints and technology are possible explanations for reduced social interactions on campus where emails or texts have become a more convenient means of communication.

Campus Use

Habitual activity including rest and socialization was described in the survey results. Students offered similar responses about eating and relaxing outside during nice weather. They also had positive feelings matching responses on overall wellbeing, when asked to assess their level of enjoyment at college. Like most students, these participants communicated feeling equally stressed and optimistic about college.

Focus Group Analysis

Two focus groups were held at the BCC with a total of ten participants. Sessions were structured as a 45-minute walking tour and a group conversation on campus design. Audio recordings were transcribed and coded. The content was reviewed and grouped according to themes that emerged from commentary on aspects of campus design. From that, six codes were identified:

Student Profile
Social Interactions
Campus Engagement
Traditional Campus Design
Comfort
Stress

Three themes that emerged from these codes included Scholarly Identity, Belonging, and Wellbeing.

Scholarly Identity

Thinking about the college experience, Lewis and Jackson (2014) suggest, "not all students . . . have fully embraced a scholarly identity and developed aspirations for high levels of academic achievement" (p. 31). To understand how scholarly identity is constructed, more information is needed regarding variables involved. Aspects of identity formation likely include social networks based on common goals and shared interests that support scholarship.

Student Profile

When participants were asked if they enjoyed being a student, responses varied.

> *Some of the resources offered do not align with my needs*
> —Participant # 1

Attending school with a full-time job makes this student feel like she is missing out. In that regard, even if BCC offers a comprehensive set of resources that support students with academic needs, attending classes at night or on weekends limits access to administrative offices and social events on campus. After a day of work, this student described night classes as being "*a bit strenuous*" compared to online classes, which she prefers. In NYC, attending a campus means navigating densely populated urban areas and public transportation. Commuter students who are employed may be less likely to attend day classes, meet with fellow students for campus events, or talk with faculty during office hours. There are certainly alternatives available, such as online classes or email communication, though those options also come with a degree of social isolation. This is less of an issue for students with flexible schedules, enrolled in daytime courses and solely focused on academics.

Participants talked about the experience of being a college student:

> *It gives a different view from high school education*
>
> —Participant # 2

> *I took a break from school for like three years but then I got tired of being a cashier at Wholefoods, so I just came back.*
>
> —Participant # 3

The former statement compares college to secondary education whereas the latter recalls hardship in the workforce. Both compare past and present, acknowledging fulfillment they experience as a student. Interestingly, none of the participants were the first to attend college in their family, referencing graduates from their extended family. One female student even identified herself as a legacy student since both her mother and father had graduated from BCC.

Social Interactions

Thinking about the social dimensions of the academic environment, Boyer's (1987) research on the undergraduate experience reminds us, "students need solitude and intimacy as well as togetherness; and they should be able to choose their companions without institutional constraint" (p. 187). During the focus group, participants were asked to discuss the type and frequency of social interactions they experienced on campus with questions related to friends, classmates, and time spent on campus. Friendship and routine are formed by built environment in that shared classes and free time facilitate social engagement in busy academic schedules.

Alone

About half of respondents described a more solitary experience on campus:

> *Most of the time I'm alone because I'm usually just going to classes then going home*
>
> —Participant # 4

> *I'm usually sitting alone on the phone*
>
> —Participant # 5

No, I have classmates that I like a lot, but I don't have friends on campus. I don't just hang on campus. I don't have time.
—Participant # 1

Classmates

Students categorized classmates as anyone they work with to complete assignments or review coursework.

So, I have classmates who I spend time with but after class you'll be like 'did you hear what the teacher said? Blah blah blah—OK bye' and we don't see each other, and we don't talk
—Participant # 5

Yeah . . . I'm one of those people that has a group chat, and we keep each other posted and we let each other know about the classwork that's due and we do work together
—Participant # 3

I don't have friends-friends, but I do have class friends and it's like a combination of ideas in the beginning. But, in my Statistics class, which is very hard class, there are students around me that don't understand so I don't let them copy but I'll explain it to them, and we do it together. But that always happens inside the classroom like ten minutes before teacher comes in.
—Participant # 1

Figure 4.6 The Quad and Gould Hall Memorial Library (Bronx Times)

Saltrick (1996) argues that "college for many of us is a process of socialization... [t]he strength of the future physical university lies less in pure information and more in collage as community" (p. 31). Appropriately, a multitude of communities seem to exist within the academic environment, defined by various degrees of social interaction that produce different types of relationships.

Friends

Students describe friendship on campus:

> *I do have like friends on campus, like from last semester but it's so hard to keep up because last semester we had one class together. We meet up in North Hall or even in Colston Hall. That's it*
>
> —Participant # 3

> *I think it was last semester, I had a break in between class; like my first class was at 10am and my next one was at like 3pm. So, I met some friends, and we would get a room in the library and study and stuff*
>
> —Participant # 2

> *I'm with friends because when I'm alone, I'm usually studying inside... I eat with my friends at the tables. If I'm outside eating, I am definitely with friends.*
>
> —Participant # 4

Figure 4.7 Students on the Quad (BCC Flickr, 2018c, May 10)

The role of contact in relationship building is reiterated in Deasy's (1974) findings at the University of Chicago where "in an analysis of friendship . . . closeness or proximity was found to be precisely correlated to recognition and liking," reinforcing the idea that regular interactions create shared experience that increases potential for bonding (p. 49).

For them, passively engaging with their surroundings could involve just being on the phone. Limited time on campus was another point made, regarding the challenges of spending time with classmates on campus, despite connecting in class. Participants saw classmates as people they met in a lecture or worked with to complete assignments.

During our conversation, students defined their range of social encounters. In some instances, regular interactions in class could strengthen the connection between students, ultimately shifting the label of classmate to friend; however, differing course schedules hindered the ability to stay in regular contact. These friendships were nurtured by coordinating class schedules and using breaks between classes to reunite, although time was spent completing coursework as opposed to planning to socialize off campus. Whereas others viewed time spent with friends as leisurely, citing time outside or eating together as social moments on campus. The distinction between scholarly and social aspects of campus life were distinguished by working independent in the library versus relaxing with friends outside.

Belonging

In "The Humanistic Psychology of Metapsychology" (1981), Giorgi examines the relationship between place and space asserting, "there are ways in which man belongs to the world, or the soul belongs to the body, or the public is related to the private, that the analytic style of thinking cannot capture because it presupposes the cutting off of the belonging relationships" (p. 40). He notes dimensions in the social fabric of a space, additionally how that can be interpreted as belonging. The concept of social belonging relates to postsecondary education because it creates a foundation for the academic experience. Walton and Cohen (2007) describe it as a central human need to have positive relationships with others. Research suggests that students who occupy minority identities are more likely to experience some level of uncertainty in academic environments that could potentially affect performance or overall wellness. Campuses that encourage social belonging are also better at supporting their students' quality of life, particularly those with complex social identities.

Incidentally, focus group participants were unanimous on feeling welcome on campus. Student commentary highlighted the possibilities in this landscape alluding to Gibson's (1986) concept of *affordances* or "what (an) object offers the animal, what it provides or furnishes, either good or ill"

(p. 127). Student also referred to *positive affordances,* places where users go unnoticed so they can relax or simply disappear within green spaces on campus (Gibson, 1986, p. 143).

Some students share vivid descriptions of belonging on campus.

> *People just be on the grass doing whatever they want. I remember one time I saw this guy doing yoga on the grass and was like "oh that's cool"*
> —Participant # 6

> *There's nothing menacing about it, I don't know it just seems very calm. Like if I want to sit here, I can.*
> —Participant # 7

Participants characterized the green spaces on campus as places where people are free, reminiscent of the campus culture of the sixties, a time when ideas were exchanged, and shared experience was valued.

The area located directly in front of the North Hall building has four benches that provides a direct view of the major green spaces on campus, in addition to the Gould Memorial Library. Participants identified this specific place and building as having the most meaning for them on campus because the space outside the North Hall acts like a front porch as well as a home turf, a place to connect with friends between classes. As Deasy and Lasswell

Figure 4.8 Students on the Quad (BCC Flickr, 2018b, May 3)

suggest (1985), "if there is a place to stand outside the flow of traffic, or even better a comfortable place to sit down, social contact develops. If this kind of event recurs regularly, a social center is born" (p. 129).

Campus Engagement

The varying degrees of closeness we have with others is defined by "minor conversational routines," seemingly fleeting and inconsequential interactions that influence the campus experience (Collins, 2004, p. 18). When asked about talking with faculty in outside areas on campus, participants explained they offer a quick "*hello*" or avoid eye contact all together. Alternately, when asked about friendships on campus, students made two distinctions namely being friendly in class versus having genuine friendships with classmates, although they explained when the shared class is over, staying close can pose a challenge. In some instances, interactions were often downgraded to text messages of "*hey, how are you doing?*"

Traditional Campus Design

The discussion of campus in spatial terms recalled Hall's (1966) concept of *sociofugal* and *sociopetal* design, which offered further insight on the

Figure 4.9 Pathways at BCC (F. Blanchard, 2017, June 12)

student experience (p. 146). In that, one problematic issue identified relates to the ease with which students can physically access the campus, as a participant explains:

> *I have to walk a whole twenty minutes to get here and sometimes, because it's very far, most of the time you want to attend class but because of the distance, you're like NO, you're not going to class. When I was a freshman, I had to look for the buildings and I was a whole hour late. And it got me pissed.*
>
> —Participant # 4

This student expressed frustration due to the shift from dense grid-like organization in the urban environment (*sociofugal*) to the expanse of space found in campus landscape, where people are brought together at specific junctures (*sociopetal*) as seen in Figure 4.4.

In contrast, other students were quite positive about specific aspects of the campus design.

> *I do like my campus, and it looks better than most campuses for a community college.*
>
> —Participant # 2

> *I thoroughly enjoy the campus, it's on top of a hill which means you have to go up some very huge steps or from the side, but I ride my bike*

Figure 4.10 Bronx Community College (BCC Flickr, 2009b, September 10)

> *in so it's nice to be able to come in through here (pointing to the side of the campus) and I also appreciate that there are lots of places to park my bike and lock it up and that's everywhere.*
>
> —Participant # 1

> *I do like the campus; I like that it used to be NYU's campus and like this North Hall is one of the newest buildings. It looks nice to me.*
>
> —Participant # 3

Responses indicate students are proud of the aesthetic at their campus, especially when they compare it to the average community college. They also referenced the prestige of inheriting their campus from NYU, emphasizing the idea campus landmarks are a source of legacy that bind students together in a shared identity derived from the institution, one defined by scholarship (Dober, 1992).

Many students identified the North Hall and Library building as being their favorite location on campus along with the quad located in the center of the campus. One student referenced her most cherished aspect of the campus:

> *The fact that I feel like I'm at an actual college away from the Bronx*
>
> —Participant # 6

This comment highlights critical aspects of the campus in terms of location and experience because the student derives a sense of pride from the traditional design at her college, which supports her scholarly identity and the feeling of belonging at BCC.

Beyond the experience of entering a space that transports students beyond the Bronx, like the Greek concept of an oasis located outside the metropolis, this campus is designed for learning with aesthetic qualities that encourage contemplation and solitude. When asked about their concept of a traditional campus, participants referenced the importance of timeless visuals that provide a unique lived environment, positive characteristics of design they identified as being essential to the experience of BCC's campus. These observations are demonstrated in Image 4.5.

When asked to describe a traditional campus, student responses varied:

> *I imagine it looks a lot like this one with benches, with clear pathways to each building. Everything looks well kept*
>
> —Participant # 7

> *I think this looks like how other colleges look and I feel like it gives me the feeling like I'm away when I'm here.*
>
> —Participant # 3

Figure 4.11 Gould Memorial Library (J. Hill, 2017a, October 16)

Participant descriptions were reminiscent of Olmsted's belief that a campus should have "a suitable degree of seclusion and a suitable degree of association . . . [because] the heated, noisy life of a large town is obviously not favorable to the formation of habits of methodical scholarship" (National Park Service, 2021). Students defined a traditional academic environment in terms of functionality, precision, and experience. One identified the importance of a spatial plan that is logically organized for comfortable movement between buildings. The second referenced the feeling of being "away" setting the campus apart from the outside world. The concept of being "away" can refer to relief from the city or feeling outside the daily grind. For these students, campus design supports their ability to reflect on both life and learning. Here a sense of tradition is embraced through design, one that offers students membership to a larger community of scholars.

Wellbeing

Academically, a community college is the middle ground between high school and university, a new academic landscape with equally new challenges. Many students struggle to navigate this environment which oftentimes can be the product of insufficient academic and emotional support or even a lack of representation on campus. Here, some pursue a terminal degree that will prepare them for the workforce where others complete the first half of a four-year journey. Regardless of one's trajectory, wellbeing can determine success on these pathways as Dyment and Bell (2007), posit that "green school grounds are more inclusive of people who may feel isolated on the basis of gender, class, race and ability suggesting that these spaces promote, in a very broad sense, social inclusion" (169).

Comfort

Inside Buildings

Students were asked to use word association to explore the experiential aspects of the campus design. This method was employed by Cooper-Marcus and Wischemann (1998) in their research at Berkeley University, a study that examined the relationship between campus design, mental health, and emotional wellbeing.

Figure 4.12 Colston Hall (M. Burger, 2017, October 15)

Figure 4.13 Bronx Community College Library Interior (T. Mayo, 2017, October 15)

These words were associated to the feeling of being indoors on campus, responses were as follows:

> *It kind of depends on the building. When I go to the library, and I go to the second floor I feel COMFORTABLE and SPACIOUS and GOOD*
> —Participant # 2

> *When I'm in Colston or Language Hall or Bliss, I feel CLAUSTRO-PHOBIC because it's very DARK. It feels like the paint is really dark and it's chipping, it's COLD. It just feels CLOSED IN.*
> —Participant # 4

> *It makes me feel like I am really COMFORTABLE when I am in North Hall (and Library Building) like I am really GLAD to be here but when I'm in the other ones I'm like ready to go.*
> —Participant # 4

Positioned at the north end of the campus where students both enter and exit, the North Hall and Library building embodies the concept of a "front yard." These narratives expose how the aesthetic qualities of this familiar place can decrease the amount of stress students experience.

The social experience of being inside buildings:

> *I'm someone who likes to stay indoors so the time it gets to me . . . I get STRESSED because I don't get to talk to a lot of people and when I go to the canteen, I see a lot of people and even though I don't really have conversations with them the little noise I hear makes me feel more COMFORTABLE.*
> —Participant # 4

For this student, Cooper-Marcus and Wischemann's (1998) concept of home turf or home base is realized in the canteen where she experiences acceptance, comfort, and belonging. In the canteen, she has created community.

Participants explained they felt comfortable and focused inside the North Hall and Library building, used as a basis of comparison for other buildings in that it felt both open and new. Constructed in 2012, it is the most recent addition to the campus. Negative sentiments were conveyed in descriptions of older buildings, where the interior and lighting seem darker due to an infrastructure they felt was less well-maintained.

Outside Buildings

Students shared words that described the experience of being in outdoor spaces on campus:

> *Usually for me it would be HAPPY like when I have attended class . . . because I actually did it. And when you walk outside of Colston at night and there are not a lot of people on campus there is just this particular smell that is just like NATUREY, and you know you don't smell that much in the Bronx so it's very RELAXING even*
> —Participant # 1

> *Outside campus I feel like I am back to reality. I am not in class anymore and it brings everything I was thinking about back to the mind. I'd say it brings me BACK TO REALITY*
> —Participant # 4

Visual aspects of the campus produce a positive and calming effect. Kaplan and Kaplan's (1989) research considers characteristics of a restorative environment that emphasize the role of escape in the relationship between stress and natural environments not unlike the shift from a stressful class to the tranquil outdoors. Participants discussed sensory experiences such as the image and scent of nature. One student recalled the whimsical quality of the green space at BCC, stating that her experience with nature on campus is rather atypical, in the Bronx. She explained the solitude on campus was restorative for her, especially after class. Relatedly, Kaplan and Kaplan (1989) identify the restorative aspects of nature that include *"being away, extent, fascination, and compatibility"* (p. 186).

Students expressed a sense of accomplishment at the end of the day, a satisfaction that comes from completing course obligations like attending class. Once students exit buildings and enter outside areas, they tend to reflect on course discussions, experience the calm of their surroundings or allow for mental and physical readjustment. Participants shared the movement from a closed space to an open campus area is symbolic of the progress they were making toward their goals. Short-term goals include regular attendance and completing lectures versus long-term goals like finishing the semester. One student remarked on the campus by night, specifically how the trees and grass frame her engagement with nature. She referenced the uniqueness of that experience in the Bronx and the wonderment that sensation brought her, alluding to the intimacy green space offers by separating academics from everyday life.

Wellbeing

Participants highlighted several ways they engage with the campus, specifically its green spaces. Some of these interactions included consumption of food, contemplation about feelings or ideas, participating in physical activity or simply taking time to experience the serenity of the campus environment.

> *Yes, sometimes when it's nice weather I would eat my lunch outside and sit outside . . .*
>
> —Participant # 6

> *. . . it's a good place to exercise*
>
> —Participant # 2

> *I'd definitely have to say yes as well, last Fall they had a movie night here in . . . I think it's called the quad and it was so nice. I came out of class, and I saw Black Panther. Or sometimes when I come to campus early after work, I'll sit here and it's lovely and really relaxing*
>
> —Participant # 1

> *I would say yes, I like it. And I remember when they were building it (North Hall) and I would stay here for hours talking on the phone even*

Figure 4.14 North Hall (J. Hill, 2017b, October 16)

if it was cold, but I do enjoy just sitting here. And it makes you feel like you're outside the state also.
—Participant # 4

In terms of campus culture, comments suggest that this green space has some restorative characteristics as a location for social events and solitude. The green space encourages physical activity, social interaction, passive observation, and quiet contemplation. Responses indicate a distinct freedom to be alone or with others when they are outside.

The quad is where participants spent time outdoor since they like to do homework or eat in this space while sitting at the benches that surround the grassy area located at the center of the campus. This area, plus the seating around the quad itself, increases the likelihood of what Cooper-Marcus and Wischemann (1998) term "collegial encounters" because students have an insider experience resulting from the campus design exemplified by the quad or the area surrounding it. The authors refer to these spaces as a back yard because they allow for an intimate type of fraternization.

> *I like seeing people pass when I'm on the phone or I spend time on the sides on those chairs*
>
> —Participant # 3

> *I also spend time by the tables over there or sometimes in the quad. But sometimes the quad is full so I'll sit at the tables, but I also like the tables a lot more because I can do homework outside if it's nice*
>
> —Participant # 5

> *I usually spend time at the benches right in front of the café because I don't really hangout over here but sometimes when I get lunch I sit outside*
>
> —Participant # 6

Accordingly, Kaplan and Kaplan (1989) suggest that directed attention is a necessary component to plan or process information; however, this level of prolonged focus causes one to experience fatigue, not unlike that of a student who may be overthinking content after class. It is his belief that natural environments, like green spaces, allow one to disengage from directed attention thereby engaging in the process of recovery. Similarly, he discusses the role of hard fascination, passively watching something stimulating like a fast-moving vehicle, versus the soft fascination found in natural settings that provide a restorative experience. Reflection is possible because ideas are processed in the previous directed attention stage. Students consistently mentioned the quad, a place they felt at ease, spent time alone, or waited for friends. This central grassy location provides respite and connection with friends. Pathways that surround the quad, allow students to be passive observers, while benefiting from the tranquility of the green space.

For these reasons, students were asked about what they do and where they go outdoor on campus.

> *Sometimes after class I'll stay and wait for my friends to come, and I am also usually sitting and eating lunch*
>
> —Participant # 3

> *... I like sitting in the Hall of Fame and reading the plaques or I am by the cannon over there. I just like it.*
>
> —Participant # 1

As demonstrated by students in both the survey and focus group, the Hall of Fame acts as a back yard on campus because it is enclosed and therefore intimate by nature (Cooper-Marcus & Wischemann, 1998). This area serves a dual purpose by bringing people together and allowing them to stand apart from the crowd. These comments reflect an array of outdoor

Figure 4.15 Hall of Fame (BCC Flickr, 2009a, October 20)

activities students engage in and places they return to when they are on campus. While BCC has a unique campus, understanding this feedback gives more insight on the needs of community college students in general and ways design can attend to them.

References

American Association of Community Colleges. (2021). *Fast facts*. Retrieved from www.aacc.nche.edu/research-trends/fast-facts/ (accessed August 30, 2021).

Blanchard, F. (2017, June 12). *Pathways at Bronx Community College* [Photo]. Bronx, NY: Bronx Community College. Retrieved from http://counterlightsrantsandblather1.blogspot.com/2017/06/bronx-community-college-2017.html

Boyer, E. (1987). *College: The undergraduate experience in America*. New York, NY: Harper & Row Publishers.

Bronx Community College. (2009a, October 20). *Hall of fame for great Americans* [Photo]. Bronx, NY: Author. Retrieved from https://flickr.com/photos/bronxcommunitycollege/14993948539

Bronx Community College. (2009b, September 10). *Campus sky view* [Photo]. Bronx, NY: Author. Retrieved from https://flickr.com/photos/bronxcommunitycollege/51155385447

Bronx Community College. (2018a). Facts and figures. *CUNY PMP Report*. Retrieved from www.bcc.cuny.edu/about-bcc/facts-figures/ (accessed March 17, 2020).

Bronx Community College. (2018b, May 3). *Students on the quad* [Photo]. Bronx, NY: Author. Retrieved from https://flickr.com/photos/bronxcommunitycollege/50223569662

Bronx Community College. (2018c, May 10). *Students on the quad* [Photo]. Bronx, NY: Author. Retrieved from https://flickr.com/photos/bronxcommunitycollege/50238443477

Bronx Community College. (2019, October 15). Focus Group.

Burger, M. (2017, October 15). *Colston hall* [Photo]. Bronx, NY: Bronx Community College. Retrieved from www.flickr.com/photos/jag9889/26132274779

Collins, R. (2004). *Ritual interactions*. Princeton, NJ: Princeton University Press.

Cooper-Marcus, C., & Wischemann, T. (1998). Campus outdoor spaces. In C. C. Marcus & C. Francis (Eds.), *People places: Design guidelines for urban open space*. New York, NY: John Wiley & Sons.

Deasy, M. (1974). *Design for human affairs*. New York, NY: Halsted Press.

Deasy, M., & Lasswell, T. E. (1985). *Designing places for people: A handbook on human behavior for architects, designers, and facility managers*. New York, NY: Watson-Guptill.

Dober, R. (1992). *Campus design*. New York, NY: John Wiley & Sons.

Dyment, J. E., & Bell, A. (2007). Grounds for movement: Green school grounds as sites for promoting physical activity. *Health Education Research, 23*, 952–962.

Gibson, J. (1986). *The ecological approach to visual perception*. Hillsdale, NJ: Lawrence Erlbaum Associates Publishers.

Giorgi, A. P. (1981). Humanistic psychology and metapsychology. In J. R. Royce & L. P. Mos (Eds.), *Humanistic psychology. PATH in psychology*. Boston, MA: Springer.

Hall, E. (1966). *The hidden dimension: An anthropologist examines man's use of space in public and private*. New York, NY: Anchor Books.

Hill, J. (2017a, October 16). *Gould memorial library* [Photo]. Bronx, NY: Bronx Community College. Retrieved from www.flickr.com/photos/archidose/37741026151

Hill, J. (2017b, October 16). *North hall* [Photo]. Bronx, NY: Bronx Community College. Retrieved from www.flickr.com/photos/archidose/37741026151

Kaplan, S., & Kaplan, R. (1989). *Cognition and environment: Functioning in an uncertain world*. Ann Arbor, MN: Ulrich Books.

Lewis, C., & Jackson, J. (2014). Developing a scholarly identity mindset: An afterword to the special issue. *Black History Bulletin, 77*(1), 31–33.

Mayo, T. (2017, October 15). *Bronx Community College library interior* [Photo]. Bronx, NY: Bronx Community College. Retrieved from www.flickr.com/photos/obsessivephotography/37694298186

National Park Service. (2021). *The Olmsted firm-college campuses*. Retrieved from www.nps.gov/articles/000/olmsted-college-campuses.htm (accessed August 10, 2021).

Saltrick, S. A. (1996). Campus of our own: Thoughts of a reluctant conservative. *Change, 28*(2), 58–62.

Schneps Media. (2016, November 13). *Bronx Community College opens new quad* [Photo]. Bronx, NY: Bronx Community College. Retrieved from www.bxtimes.com/bronx-community-college-opens-new-quad/

Walton, G. M., & Cohen, G. L. (2007). A question of belonging: Race, social fit, and achievement. *Journal of Personality and Social Psychology, 92*, 82–96.

5 Looking Forward

Outcomes and Implications for Future Campus Design and Development

This research provides key findings about the relationship between campus design and student experience. As stated in Chapter 3, this study focused on the following central questions:

1. How does campus design impact the student experience at a community college?
2. Does contact with green space on campus provide a restorative experience and relief from the fatigue caused by directed attention?
3. Does campus design contribute to the development of a scholarly identity?

At Bronx Community College (BCC), campus design influences student experience in a variety of ways. Participant feedback unearthed several themes, chief among them, time. In New York, the average commuter student who attends community college has limited free time as employment or household responsibilities compete with academics. In that way, the gridlock and crowds further influence lived experience which means for students BCC is something of an oasis. Stress was an important topic in the focus group discussion where students described how restorative aspects of campus design brought relief when alone or with friends. Traditional design contributed to the feeling of "being away," which both reduced stress and contributed to overall wellbeing. Relatedly, participants expressed a distinct pride for being a student at this campus, which also caused them to reflect on time they had spent in the workforce. Academic setting and commitment to scholarship were foundational to the construction of scholarly identity. Applying these findings to a broader context, this chapter explores some central themes related to the community college campus.

DOI: 10.4324/9781003130598-5

Time

Employing various methods of data collection offered valuable information about this environment. To that end, time was a significant theme in both the survey and focus group. For a commuter student, a demanding schedule can greatly influence the ability to engage with the institution, such as the setting and campus life. As discussed, community college students often complete a degree in addition to part-time or full-time employment, which affects movement through academic spaces. The survey results revealed that students do spend time on campus as well as outside and near green spaces, yet they usually report spending that time in a purposeful manner, an important observation in campus use at a commuter school.

In terms of design, the campus communicates with users through architecture, maintenance, and landscape. These aspects of design contribute to positive interactions within campus buildings and outside areas. During the focus group, students described feeling comfortable in the North Hall and Library building as the product of well-lit classrooms and modern facilities. Similarly, the aesthetic qualities of campus outdoor space feel supportive evidenced by the benches lining the quad. These areas have great appeal to students because they are ideal for groups and being alone.

To better understand how students develop a sense of belonging, this research utilized a form trace analysis during the focus group that encouraged students to share ways they spend time on campus. Cooper-Marcus and Wischemann's (1998) research at Berkeley reminds us "the need to feel that one belongs to one spot is so compelling that most students, even those with no formal tie to any single building (i.e., those who had not yet chosen a major) still appropriated a place to which they returned daily" (p. 177). The home turf orients the student within campus design by creating a space they can personalize and thereby feel intimacy within the greater college environment. At BCC these concepts proved accurate with 85 percent of students who identified as having a specific place they visited regularly. Areas on campus most referenced included the North Hall and Library building, the Hall of Fame for Great Americans, and the benches that line green spaces on campus. In this instance, the North Hall and the Hall of Fame constitute the home turf, where the benches are considered a front porch. Furthermore, as discussed in Chapter 4, Deasy and Lasswell (1985) propose where there are areas that allow users to step outside the natural flow of traffic with the possibility to sit or stand, there exists the potential for social connection within the "social center" that has been created (p. 129). In the case of BCC, students describe a nucleus in these areas with benches, one that constitutes the heart of the campus organism. Focus group participants spoke about spent time on campus and how BCC's campus design made them feel.

> *I feel like this is the closest campus that looks like a real campus in CUNY, but that's just my opinion*
> —Participant # 3

> *Last semester, I had a class and I had to spend like until 8pm over here. And that was my first time seeing how nice the green area was. I sat here until I think 10pm . . . I had music in my ear, and it made me clear like a little bit of stuff in my head. And looking up like other people will come . . . I thought I was the only person having problems . . . (but I saw) everybody was having problems. That made me feel like a little bit good about myself.*
> —Participant # 4

These responses indicate belonging, reinforced by thoughtful design. For these students, more classical aspects of the design represent a traditional college experience that takes place in an oasis. The campus at BCC conveys a freedom and accessibility these students have clearly embraced.

Time on campus unearths greater insight into the nature of belonging as well as the ability to reduce stress and actively attend to wellbeing. When asked about stress at college, survey responses included a range of "sometimes," "regularly," and "pretty often" that totaled 71 percent. Routine contact with green space appeared positively correlated to relief from fatigue, the basis of Attention Restoration Theory. Thus, student feedback reiterates engagement with campus green space feels relaxing before and after class. They are calm and inclusive.

> *There is just this particular smell that is just like nature, and you know you don't smell that much in the Bronx so it's very relaxing even*
> —Participant # 1

> *Or sometimes when I come to campus early after work, I'll sit here and it's lovely and really relaxing.*
> —Participant # 2

These comments exemplify Kaplan and Kaplan's (1989) concept of *soft fascination*, part of the restorative experience that allows the mind to recover from stress.

In thinking about the relationship between campus design and scholarly identity, students expressed regular use of the campus grounds while attending classes or using resources such as the library. In the focus group, participants were asked to elaborate further on their student experience. Relationships with other students, either friendships or classmates focused on group work, guided how time was spent on campus. Students also mentioned gathering on campus for informal and formal meetings to support each other with coursework. They shared instances of waiting for friends at the entrance of buildings either before and after class or connecting between classes during breaks. Meetings were possible due to the open design of the college.

The Oasis

A second central theme that arose during the study was the concept of an oasis, a respite from the outside world. This notion dates to the archetypal image of an academy that is physically removed and therefore separate from the metropolis. Reminiscent of the learning environment defined in Ancient Greece, medieval England, and the American Ivy League. Students expressed a great affinity for aspects of nature that define BCC's campus, specifically the green space and its ability to create a sense of place independent from overdeveloped views that define other parts of the Bronx. For these students, the oasis can influence state of mind, in that it affords intimacy by day and calm by night. Several students explained how they linger on benches, using their phone, waiting for classmates, or spending time alone. BCC students described their comfort inside the campus environment, as well as a disconnectedness that results from weak social networks at college. This notion was referenced earlier in the discussion of time spent on campus.

As a commuter school, students have varying schedules in addition to increased familial and financial responsibilities common to low-income households. These participants identified themselves as being part of a broader family structure where higher education is accessible. However, the experience of attending college has not yet been standardized for all members of their community, which means the social aspects of college are likely new and less of a priority when compared to achieving academic success. In contrast, those campuses which offer housing facilities also create more opportunities to build strong social networks. Regular time spent on campus allows students to develop support networks that extend beyond practical needs such as course assignments. Student-led organizations, like the Greek system, encourage members to bond through shared identity. For many of us, the time spent at college felt like being in a magical bubble that lasted for a few precious years. And over time, social networks emerged that continued into the professional world characterizing Bourdieu's concept of cultural capital or affiliations, knowledge, and access that position one advantageously in society.

Uses of Green Space

Considering the rarity that is green space in metropolitan settings or the endless vertical growth that has come to define modern cities, nestled in the heart of the Bronx, BCC offers students a unique college experience with its traditional campus design. Once known for its abundance of space and its old-time charm, today many parts of the Bronx are covered in blocks of similar-looking mid-sized buildings devoted to low-income housing. Like most neighborhoods in the outer boroughs surrounding New York City, the Bronx is composed of residential and commercial areas. Conversely, the campus at BCC exists in stark contrast to that dense urban aesthetic, reinforcing the unexpectedness of its campus experience. Particularly in comparison to other community colleges located in residential or suburban areas that are often less developed than the city. In these spaces, it seems safe to assume there would also be more evidence of nature, yet that is not always the case. Nassau Community College located in the suburbs of New York offers an alternative example of campus design with 225 acres of land, it is the largest community college campus in New York State (NCC, 2020). However, this campus is surprisingly car-centric with an expansive parking lot that largely informs user experience. In many ways, the design choices at this campus reflect common features of suburbia such as functionality, austerity and the automobile.

According to Dober (1992), the landscape of a campus can be incongruent to the area that surrounds it, as seen in the example of Nassau Community College, where uniformity that defines the aesthetic is part of "the democratization of land ownership" (p. 188). At the same time, this College has employed innovative methods to incorporate aspects of the early landscape using plant materials native to Long Island namely a 19 acre-tract on the college grounds that are identified as part of the original grass prairie that covered the island (Dober, 1992, p. 233). As a result, the green space at this campus contrasts with BCC's unexpected traditional design, in that NCC showcases grassy areas that, unlike the rest of suburbia, are less manicured and tamed. Embracing the natural aspects of the local landscape is good practice since it preserves indigenous plant life while diversifying the visual dimensions of campus design. Often campuses make planting choices based on budget allowances that cover the cost of maintenance. NCC presents a unique opportunity to evaluate the potential benefits of landscape preservation and advantages associated with using plant life native to the area versus investing in more conventional options that could be more expensive to maintain.

Further comparison can be drawn to other campuses located outside of the New York City area with a significant commuter student population.

A prime example is SUNY at Old Westbury, also located in Nassau County on Long Island; it spans 605 acres of sprawling green space (SUNY Old Westbury, 2020). A defining feature of this campus, which presents like a State Park, is that it is largely composed of unused green space with an almost decorative quality that encourages observation rather than engagement.

The main campus buildings are situated at the center of the grounds which are pristine, though generally untouched by students, administration, and faculty. This lack of use is reinforced by the absence of benches found beyond the main building or a well-defined campus center like the quad at BCC or the historic Rotunda and Lawn at UVA. As a result, many commuter students can be found sitting in their cars before and after class. In the absence of a designated nucleus, students park their cars in a lot located in front of the main campus building, where they listen to music or talk on their phone. In the example of Old Westbury, there is no shortage of green space, yet without clear cues of how to use the space, students interpret the greenery as a mere visual component of their campus, as opposed to an area that can be used.

The State University of New York (SUNY) system is composed of a collection of colleges with a standard campus design and a vast amount of green space. These institutions were established in locations where land was readily available, unlike colleges at CUNY which are situated in New York City. At SUNY New Paltz, a rural campus that is 257 acres in size, space is used very differently (SUNY New Paltz, 2020). At this campus, diversity is evident in its design. The most noticeable choice is the combination of institutional red brick buildings, featured throughout the SUNY system, and others that have a more eccentric modern design to complement the natural features of the rural landscape. One special aspect of the natural setting is the lake which further diversifies the layout. At SUNY New Paltz the campus has a center. Pathways guide the user through its grounds and though there is little seating near green spaces or the lake, the small scale of the campus offers a more intimate feeling compared to the sprawl found at SUNY Old Westbury. A closeness that likely translates into a positive lived experience during the academic year.

Future Areas of Analysis

In this exploration of campus design and the role of green space, some questions arose regarding different academic environments.

On-Campus Housing

Not having a dormitory at BCC influences the campus experience because student use is limited to business hours during the week. Access to administrative buildings is reduced on weekends as is the library, cafeteria, and greater open spaces. At a four-year college that provides housing, students are likely moving through spaces with greater frequency, which leaves room for a combination of purposeful and purposeless activity. A significant part of the social experience is based on the idea of simply "hanging around" or "lounging" in indoor and outdoor open areas. It might be beneficial to compare the use of green space at a college where students have the option to commute or live on campus. To learn more about the development of scholarly identity, belonging, and wellbeing in terms of green space, the sample population should be as varied as possible to assess a diverse set of experiences.

Faculty and Staff

Another area of exploration could be faculty perception of campus design. These data could provide greater insight from an academic and social context. Moreover, there may be some overlap between ways students and faculty engage with space that could potentially inform future studies along with to higher education policy. The open-concept office space is popular in many academic departments because it encourages mingling between faculty and establishes easier contact with students. Similarly, quads and gardens offer that same opportunity for social engagement outdoors. These types of settings make interactions less formal and perhaps more organic. An innovative example of outdoor campus design can be found at another CUNY school located in Long Island City, Queens, a place where factory buildings were repurposed to make LaGuardia Community College (LAGCC). Part of this campus includes the Loose-Wills Sunshine Biscuit factory building, purchased for expansion in the nineties (LaGuardia Community College, 2020).

Conveniently located across the river from Manhattan, previously this area of Queens was known for its warehouses and factory space though more recently, like every area situated near the city, it has undergone major development and urbanization. At LAGCC, the courtyard in the E Building is a perfect example of a retroactive addition of green space that provides a cozy outdoor area to maximize the built environment. At this college students, faculty, staff, and administration enjoy this outdoor area equipped with benches, grass, and trees. It is a space that invites people to stay and is strategically placed on the first floor with the courtyard positioned near the cafeteria it aligns directly with the nucleus of the floor plan, which makes it feel like a classic quad at a traditional campus regardless of the industrial landscape that defines the area.

Landmarks

This study focused on how campus design, specifically green space, guides experience; however, future research could go beyond that. For example, many students identified the Hall of Fame for Great Americans as a location they frequent regularly, a concrete area that overlooks the Bronx and offers a view of green space. This was an interesting observation because the built environment provides access to visual aspects of nature, while its location behind Gould Memorial Library is secluded enough for students to gather in small groups or be alone in an otherwise densely populated borough. Students who attend community colleges in urban settings may not engage with the campus environment in the same way as students who are at schools that have a more traditional design and are located in less developed areas. Some aspects include non-academic social interactions that foster the development of strong social ties related to fraternities, extracurriculars, or campus events that connect students to a place. The traditional student often considers the postsecondary environment as a place of legacy, identity, and community that comprises their sense of belonging. This is an area of research worth further exploring because it can provide a better understanding of the essential elements required for a positive student experience.

Demographics

Age and student status are equally important factors in this analysis because younger students usually attend school on a full-time basis at traditional campuses. Perhaps, future research in this area should examine how these factors impact experience. At BCC, survey and focus group participants largely represented students between 18 and 20 years of age. As a result, this may have influenced the high occurrence of "sometimes" as a response to many questions on the survey, though a diverse age range may have revealed more definitive perceptions of campus design. Additionally, a younger student who has recently completed secondary education could arrive at a postsecondary institution with inherent bias on how physical space effects experience. This student could instinctively compare the college campus with the high school environment as evidenced by a participant in Chapter 4. Alternately, a recent high school graduate may have an overly optimistic view of the campus design, particularly in an urban area where excess space is rare. To that end, a diverse sample group will likely include a range of perspectives based on age, student status, and experience. Other areas of consideration include gender and major, as participants in this study represented a female majority that were majoring in Liberal Arts. At another campus, this may not be the case and thus a compelling point of comparison.

Community

Thinking about the impact of campus design on student experience, it is necessary to consider population and needs. At BCC, students generally work while they study and rely on fininacial aid. In their everyday lives, stress goes beyond academic challenges. At this Hispanic Serving Institution with students from underserved communities that have been historically marginalized, access to green space in the learning environment becomes an issue of social justice. To reflect on the visual qualities of private institutions like Yale calls to mind images of the monastic design for solitude in nature. Similarly, other quintessential examples of design include Olmsted's Central Park, known for its endless quality that makes it possible to get lost in nature. With a diverse collection of greenery and its complex use of space, Central Park produces the feeling of fascination and wonder. The user feels like they have transcended the gridlock and crowds of the area. In both examples thoughtful attention to natural views reinforces the importance of green space, supportive of wellbeing because it transports the individual beyond their environment. These are experiential aspects of design that should be incorporated into the community college environment since, above all, it creates the foundation to stay. That very impulse to stay on campus, continue to build social networks, or further engage with academics feels like the first step to addressing wellbeing, belonging, and scholarly identity at schools like BCC.

The community college is a very particular stage of higher education because it attends to the academic and professional needs of students from the area. The built environment is intended to support the community through education, civic duty, and public service. It creates a sense of purpose and place. In the context of this book, nature makes that possible. When a college campus is focused on its design, both students and residents feel connected to that space. They are drawn to these locations through community events that integrate the campus environment into the fabric of the neighborhood. Community colleges are different from private universities, where elitism and wealth define the experience. They are also different from magical spaces like Central Park where movies are filmed, and tourists pay homage. Instead, community colleges reflect the values of its administration, faculty, and students. It is a human space made to bring people together. It is the intersection of education and the world of work.

Campus as Place

It could be helpful to understand attitudes toward the campus from the perspective of those who live on campus versus those who commute. Students who live on campus likely experience that space with more familiarity than their commuter counterparts because it is their home, a place where they build social networks, eat meals, and attend events. For them, the college campus goes beyond the lecture halls and office hours as it is central to their lived experience. Conversely, commuter students are on campus for a specific purpose, to attend a class, complete assignments, or visit offices. They set foot in that landscape for fixed moments of the day therefore it might be less appealing to eat, sit or relax outdoor on campus. That type of contact with campus design needs to be understood to create a campus experience that caters to them. Perhaps the key is figuring out how to offer a place where commuter students feel inclined to spend time, even when they do not have to stay. Instead, they choose to spend time there because the campus belongs to them. That attention to preference and use would be valuable information to incorporate in facilities management and future campus design. In a time when talk of diversity, inclusion, and safe spaces dominate the modern learning environment, outdoor spaces with access to nature could support that mission in many ways.

Oftentimes, campuses have a designated Commuter Student Office to build community amongst this population, knowing these students engage with the space very differently to their live-in counterparts. This office could be an ideal starting point for this research, which seeks to understand campus design in terms of commuter student needs. This research also lends itself to collaborative approaches that incorporate students in the research process given they are the population being studied. Participatory Action Research provides that integrated approach by studying issues from a community-centric perspective. Similarly planting and gardening groups on campus could potentially partner with urban planning or environmental psychology students to collect data from an interdisciplinary perspective as well as examine the uses of outdoor space in a comprehensive manner.

Green Spaces on Campus: Wellbeing, Belonging, and Scholarly Identity

The college's mission is reflected in the built environment. For public institutions of higher education, that mission is intrinsically tied to notions of civic duty, service, and the lifelong pursuit of knowledge. At the City University of New York (CUNY), that mission is to "provide a public first-rate education to all students, regardless of means or background," an opportunity this institution feels allows many to achieve upwards social mobility, and in that way, contributes to the growth of New York City's middle class (City University of New York 2020). It is necessary then to explore how that mission is reflected in the built environment and lived experience at its campuses. In the case of Bronx Community College, access to green space is just one way the campus upholds that commitment to excellence. Naturally, CUNY's history was always intertwined with high standards of civic duty, in that it offered the first free public higher education in America (City University of New York, 2021).

Wellbeing

Gaines (as cited in Kenney et al., 2005) explains that "sixty percent of college-bound students told the Carnegie Foundation that visual environment was the most critical factor in choosing a college" (p. 31). Academic excellence is similarly weighted to the experiential aspects of campus design. The idea is that students choose their campus as opposed to the campus choosing them. By that same logic, it is reasonable to assume the above statement refers to upper middle-class students visiting campuses with their parents, in pursuit of the right fit. The element of choice is synonymous with wealth and resources since the selection process necessitates precision and consensus. At a community college, where students come from households straddling the poverty line in underserved neighborhoods, that concept of choice is very different. In this instance, students make choices on availability and convenience since the academic experience must fit an urban lifestyle based on family responsibilities, employment, and limited financial resources. However, the wealthier student may be on to something in choosing their campus based on aesthetics when motivation and wellness are consistently linked to contact with nature or natural views. Manicured landscapes at an institution demonstrate care to the student population just as attention to the built environment communicates its mission and creates an experience that allows students to live up to its expectations.

Research has been conducted on the relationship between walking habits developed on campus and the positive health practices that continue beyond student life. Sun et al. (2015) discuss the walking behavior of students at a university in Hong Kong. This study was centered on understanding perceptions of walking by analyzing walking patterns. As mentioned in the discussion in Chapter 4 on Findings, students enter the academic environment with preconceived notions about spatial layout, academic landscapes, and comfort. One student was very vocal about her frustration in the first days on campus because being in a closed area with different buildings separated by distinct natural spaces like grassy fields made her uncomfortable, a departure from the utilitarian design of her urban high school. This is a critical point because some students may require guidance on how to engage with new spaces. When talking to a colleague about her time at Cornell University in Upstate New York, as a Latina student from the Bronx, she remembered the beautiful spaces felt so new that for some time she did not realize she could use them. This colleague described her initial engagement with campus space like being in a museum where the convention is to look but not touch.

Additionally, other forms of activity are encouraged by the campus that offers valuable access to green space, such as biking, sports, yoga, and meditation. These contribute to health and wellness in ways that attend to mental and physical aspects of development. Investing in the production and expansion of these spaces is certainly a health issue that can be implemented in the university's agenda and within the fabric of the campus culture.

Belonging

The presence of green space in campus design has proven health benefits that can also assist with social integration. College life is not just about meeting academic standards; it is also very much about occupying new spaces that form identity. Many people feel the biggest changes in their lives happened at college, when meeting different people and exchanging new ideas is commonplace, almost essential to the experience. The college environment promotes social development through design choices that demonstrate Kaplan and Kaplan's (1989) Attention Restoration Theory (ART), in terms of feeling away, rested, and open to new experiences. The occurrence of open green spaces with benches and tables presents an invitation to the user, that social dimensions of the college experience matter. Study participants described a habit of waiting for friends before and after class, hanging around the entrances or tables located near frequented buildings. Likely, most of us remember that as being a major part of high school because it felt like you belonged to a group, just as much as a place. For urban community college students, that feeling of belonging is crucial to performance and overall wellbeing.

Enhancing the number of casual encounters or home bases on campus means that students have a refuge from the weight of the outside world and classroom experience. In an environment where high-rises and concrete define the aesthetic of the metropolis, intimacy is still possible. New York has shown that to be true with thoughtful examples of place-making in Midtown at locations like Herald Square with plants interspersed between tables and chairs that act as a buffer between people and traffic, more so allowing tourists and locals alike to dine at the center of the fastest city in the world. Accordingly, the campus at BCC has some wonderful opportunities that develop casual encounters and home bases in its green space. With the world coming to a halt during the global pandemic, most capital management projects scheduled for the 2020–2021 academic year were delayed. This campus is no exception with major renovations and additions to be implemented as just another example of BCC's unrelenting commitment to its students. Some spaces that provide chances for change include the back of the famous Marcel Breuer-designed building known as Muister

Hall. This ode to contemporary art contains an interesting, closed space behind it that offers endless possibilities for place-making. Another fascinating aspect of this already unique campus design is its ability to transform despite the historically congested conditions that define New York.

Scholarly Identity

The social and emotional component of student wellbeing is directly connected to the ability to integrate within the campus landscape, to feel like you belong at college. In many ways, academic performance is founded on these aspects of the college experience which include meeting expectations and adapting to situations. With 64 percent of students enrolled on a full-time basis and 55 percent who are the first generation to attend college, BCC produces phenomenal outcomes (BCC, 2018). Known nationally for its Accelerated Study in Associate Programs (ASAP), BCC provides students with comprehensive high touch academic support from a team of staff and administration dedicated to student success. Apart from the academic side, students also receive financial support that makes the path to graduation more predictable. At the community college level, BCC is a leader in the CUNY system. These programs certainly contribute to the nationally recognized accomplishments at this campus, though its built environment can take some credit in achieving that elusive element of identity some community college campuses are missing. In this study, students acknowledged the fact that they attend a CUNY school, although they also expressed a distinct connection to BCC. They saw themselves as students of this campus, scholars that used to work at Wholefoods or employees that take classes at night. There is an identity that exists in tandem with the former high school student or part-time worker, one that makes them a learner. The physical environment reinforces that idea when sitting in the library is comfortable, walking on campus pathways after class is a source of pride or being alone on campus is a reward after a long day in the city. The space defines the experience, which means any effort to maintain and expand that chance to connect is a step toward the construction of scholarly identity. An area of study that can be furthered by learning more about students at different stages of study and life.

Looking Forward

In a post-COVID-19 context, the campus landscape has taken on new meaning. Many students feel they missed essential moments of college life that rely on contact with people and environment, built or natural. The online learning that took place during the pandemic has certainly changed our concept of connectedness, a challenging substitute for human interaction and contact with green space. At the same time, these are meaningful lessons on higher education because we have discovered that a community can begin in digital spaces and can then grow on campus. Predictably engagement with outdoor spaces does truly frame the academic experience in ways we can now quantify having spent time away, perhaps longing for a return. This is a critical moment for research on campus design; let's not wait!

References

Bronx Community College. (2018). Facts and figures. *CUNY PMP Report*. Retrieved from www.bcc.cuny.edu/about-bcc/facts-figures/ (accessed March 17, 2020).

City University of New York. (2020). *About CUNY: History*. Retrieved from www.cuny.edu/about/ (accessed January 20, 2020).

City University of New York. (2021). *CUNY digital history archive*. Retrieved from https://cdha.cuny.edu/coverage/coverage/show/id/3 (accessed November 20, 2020).

Cooper-Marcus, C., & Wischemann, T. (1998). Campus Outdoor Spaces. In Marcus, C. C., & Francis, C. *People Places: Design Guidelines for Urban Open Space*. New York, NY. John Wiley & Sons.

Deasy, M. & Laswell, T. E. (1985). *Designing places for people: A handbook on human behavior for architects, designers, and facility managers*. New York, NY: Watson-Guptill.

Dober, R. (1992). *Campus design*. New York, NY: John Wiley & Sons.

Kaplan, S. & Kaplan, R. (1989). *Cognition and Environment: Functioning in an Uncertain World*. Ann Arbor, MN: Ulrich Books.

Kenney, D. R., Dumont, R., & Kenney, G. (2005). *Mission and place: Strengthening learning and community through campus design*. Westport, CT: Praeger.

LaGuardia Community College. (2020). *Timeline*. Retrieved from www.laguardia.edu/anniversary/1980s.html (accessed January 20, 2020).

Nassau Community College. (2020). *Our history: Nassau now. Fast facts*. Retrieved from www.ncc.edu/aboutncc/fastfacts.shtml (accessed January 20, 2020).

Sun, G., Acheampong, R. A., Lin, H., & Pun, V. C. (2015). Understanding walking behavior among university students using theory of planned behavior. *International Journal of Environmental Research and Public Health*, *12*(11), 13794–13806.

SUNY New Paltz. (2020). *Campuses*. Retrieved from www.suny.edu/campuses/newpaltz/ (accessed January 21, 2020).

SUNY Old Westbury. (2020). *About us*. Retrieved from www.oldwestbury.edu/about-us (accessed January 21, 2020).

Afterword

Green space in campus design uncovers various themes in American society. From an architectural perspective, it complements the built environment, highlighting purpose and cohesion. This was the case at Harvard University where ivy unified a collection of buildings that may have appeared disconnected with newer additions to the campus layout. In terms of culture, green space plays a major role in cultivating social and experiential aspects of campus life. As discussed in the earlier chapters, the opportunities for positive interactions increase when there are areas available that support both small and big group gatherings in an outdoor context.

The greenery invites users to linger or even incorporate specific types of engagement with these spaces such as connecting with friends at the entrance or exit (front yard or backyard) of buildings or spending time in grassy enclaves while eating or resting. That concept of "staying" on campus is possible because the green space affords a range of use within campus outdoor areas, which leads to the experiential aspects of nature. The campus environment is often framed by the presence of trees, grass, gardens, water, and seating located in an open space. In that way, student users can see the institution is an experience that goes beyond brick and mortar. It is all encomposing, an oasis that extends from the lecture halls and dormitories right through to the nucleus or rather the heart of the campus, a location designed to purposely bring students together at work and play.

Keeping those ideas in mind forces us to imagine campus design as an exercise in both function and form, one that attends to different facets of the college experience. At the community college level, the campus becomes a tool for social justice by encouraging users to expect a certain standard of care from their institution, a precursor to the expectations that could be applied to their neighborhood, local community, city, and state. The nurturing aspects of contact with nature are universal in that way because they remain the same for people at any stage of life. Cultivating an appreciation for green space can be accomplished with increased engagement with sustainable practices on campus. In a time when the detrimental effects of climate change loom large in the media, knowledge, and action directed toward the preservation of green space on campus can have a far-reaching impact on civic notions of participation regarding environmental issues.

During COVID-19, the theme of access has been at the forefront of discussions on health. This has been a major concern for people from underserved neighborhoods where limited contact with green space negatively impacted quality of life during lockdown period. This example highlights the importance of green space not just in an educational context but a larger issue of access indicates care. There have been several studies on hidden bias that green spaces are meant for more affluent communities which tend to be in predominantly white areas (Davis, 2020). Likewise with increased racial and economic segregation in urban settings comes decreased access to green spaces, an indicator of disparity in terms of quality of life (Saporito & Casey, 2015). In this way, green space relates to larger issues of wellness and the distribution of resources across communities. For students to appreciate the value of green space it should be available at the postsecondary level, which is likely the terminal academic experience for many completing undergraduate or graduate studies. It is also a crucial moment when students can engage with these conversations and understand the role of conservation in terms of community wellness.

Another theme is safety, considering how well-maintained green spaces that are both open and safe can increase the value of property in an urban context versus the occurrence of parks used for illegal activity (drugs/violence) or a respite for individuals without proper access to resources like shelter. In the latter examples, these types of shared green space can devalue an area for both renters and homeowners alike. A comparative analysis of parks and safety in five US cities found that "when parks are perceived as unsafe, people are unlikely to derive the health and community benefits from them" (Williams et al., 2020). The presence and preservation of green space is an issue that needs to be examined from a broader perspective in that it indicates a range of access that also translates to high or low quality of life for members of a community. Other factors influenced by green space include air quality, gardens, vegetation, exercise, and likelihood of sustainable practices.

That said, the theme of community also emerged in this exploration of campus design. To fully understand the role of green space on campus is to examine the design features within the college landscape. As Clark Kerr (1982) put it, the modern university should be thought of as a *multiversity*, a microcosm where the larger societal framework is repeated in the form of a unique learning environment composed of students, faculty, staff, and administration. In such a space, there are certain needs that must be met to ensure the functionality of the institution and more specifically its growth. Similarly, the urban community college plays an integral role in the maintenance of a neighborhood because its student body will learn vital lessons from time spent within this multiverse, a place where essential aspects of a livable environment are learned, from a diverse interpretation of health.

Social sustainability assesses the design of the built environment with that of the social world. As a concept, it explores how an infrastructure supports the cultural and social aspects of life, social amenities, systems for citizen engagement as well as space for people and places to evolve (Colantonio & Dixon, 2009). In many ways, the college campus is constructed with those very principles in mind since higher education attends to the development of both the mind and body. Contact with the academic environment is curated by the location and experience offered while completing a degree or professional certification. Embedded in this dialogue on social sustainability is another on connectedness and accessibility.

As previously mentioned, the degree to which the campus design brings users together is just as important as being supportive of academics in that attention to community building and social identity make for meaningful shared space that can attend to a range of needs. Accessibility in the built and natural landscape emphasizes universal design and social connectedness for differently-abled users. In the urban college campus, students should have shared green spaces that encourage engagement beyond what is available in a larger city context. This type of limited access is exemplified in the New York City subway where wheelchairs and strollers are rerouted to specific stations for access to ramps and elevators, widespread universal design made impossible in one of the largest underground transportation systems in the world. Similarly, students who occupy multiple minority identities and reside in neighborhoods with less resources require these inviting shared spaces in their learning experience to witness the connection between nature, health, and community building.

With that conversation of access comes the theme of privilege. In my earlier chapter, I talked about my former colleague's experience at Cornell University and the culture shock that accompanied her initial contact with the campus space. Many of us can still recall the mix of excitement and discomfort that came with the early days of college. Simple changes required adjustment, such as the different layout from high school, a place where most classes were usually grouped together in a single building. More than that resources are spaced out over a larger surface area connected by long pathways, the landscape and architecture colliding in ways that communicate legacy.

This relates to the larger theme of belonging. In the chapter called Space Matters: Rethinking University for and with Underrepresented Students, the author explores "the often-fraught relationship between campus space and students' perception of their access, particularly first-generation college students and other populations who have been historically underrepresented at universities" (Miles, 2016, p. 16). Around the world, students are forcing institutions to remove statues of historic figures representing slavery, discrimination, and inequality that defined the past; however, there are other less tangible facets of White privilege so innocuous they quietly influence the culture of a space. North American society has historically been guided by Protestant values shaped by White men whose cultural expression has been conveyed through specific concepts of cleanliness, refinement, and prestige realized architecturally in the aesthetic of European culture. These features are echoed in revered places such as museums, universities, and parks allowing that culture of exclusion to carry over. To that extent, it becomes necessary to reimagine space in order to address a history of exclusion and renew the relationship to nature.

From the perspective of Critical Race Theory, these are examples of cultural supremacy based on constructs of whiteness. In an analysis, Kohl and Halter (2021) assert museums at their best are places that offer a space for reflection and conversation. However, at their worst they are a reminder of the power and privilege they choose to perpetuate (x), reiterating the oppressive culture that can accompany celebrated landscaped and built environments, even within typically progressive urban contexts.

In New York City, the urban context is so iconic that places like the Museum of Natural History or The Metropolitan Museum of Modern Art are known the world over. They command power not only because they house critical cultural artifacts and knowledge but also because of their built and landscaped environment. They are seen as touchstones of prestige, examples of high culture. As an educator, I have had the opportunity to visit these locations on class trips with different types of students: those who were recently arrived immigrants completing ESL courses and those in their first and second years of community college. Years later, I can still remember the challenge of visiting with young people who did not feel inherently connected to those places, sites where scores of tourists from out-of-town or well-to-do New Yorkers make their annual pilgrimage because they are drawn to these locations. It always seemed like these cultural institutions were governed by a form of racialized conduct that was further defined by social class. Standard to these visits was an older White docent who guided us through different areas largely assuming a Euro-centric cultural frame of reference in their discussion of collections. What is more, students were often scolded for using their phones or engaging with the space incorrectly (sitting down or standing too close). A hidden curriculum of conduct exists which governs culturally significant spaces thereby teaching young people how to engage with the built and landscaped environment. It could be valuable to learn more about how those rules of engagement influence contact with spaces perceived as being green and/or pristine.

To appreciate differing cultural associations with space requires further research on perception. To that end, Agyeman's (1990) article "Black People in a White Landscape: Social and Environmental Justice" considers how in Britain, Black identity and experience have been so deeply rooted in the urban context that the English countryside feels alien, if not foreboding. Here the author acknowledges nativist cultural associations connected to farming, purity, and whiteness that exist in open landscapes outside of the city limits. The concept of leisure is depicted in outdoor culture but is also often racially defined by whiteness in recreational activities such hiking or rock climbing—pastimes of the affluent white community who are represented in marketing campaigns and these picturesque locations. Nevertheless, this piece speaks to a more subtle concept regarding the appreciation of nature which has been both accepted and branded in a manner that does not include a diverse community. Venturing into open landscapes that are scenic and removed from the urban context also requires people of color to seek out spaces where they are underrepresented to the extent that safety is of concern.

The impact of historical legacy naturally appears in the lived environment. These reflections on the experience of cultural landmarks relate to green space since it speaks to the hidden privilege embedded within a supposedly shared place. The City University of New York, Bronx Community College presents an interesting example in that conversation, originally created for an affluent student body who were predominantly white and male it would eventually serve a diverse community from low-income households who are people of color and speakers of other languages. It is impossible to know whether students of today would feel welcome in the original campus in the days of NYU, however it would be worth further exploring whether that legacy of elitism remains in green space or perhaps monuments such as the Hall of Fame of Great Americans.

References

Agyeman, J. (1990). Black people in a white landscape: Social and environmental justice. *Built Environment, 16*(3), 232–236.

Colantonio, A., & Dixon, T. (2009). *Measuring socially sustainable urban regeneration in Europe.* Oxford: Oxford Institute for Sustainable Development (OISD), Oxford Brookes University.

Davis, S. (2020, July 9). Environmental racism and access to public spaces. *Dogwood Alliance*. Retrieved from: https://www.dogwoodalliance.org/2020/07/environmental-racism-and-access-to-public-spaces/. Accessed on September 10, 2020.

Kerr, C. (1982). *The uses of the university*. Cambridge, MA: Harvard University Press.

Kohl, R., & Halter, J. (2021). Challenging white supremacy: A call for critical race theory in museums. *Theory and Practice: The Emerging Museum Professionals Journal*. Vol. 4. Retrieved from: https://articles.themuseumscholar.org/2021/12/09/challenging-white-supremacy-a-call-for-critical-race-theory-in-museums/. Accessed on: December 10, 2021.

Miles, L. T. R. (2016). Space matters: Rethinking university spaces for and with underrepresented students. In J. Silverman & M. Sweeney (Eds.), *Remaking the American college campus: Essays* (pp. 15–26). Jefferson, NC. McFarland & Company, Inc. Publishers.

Saporito, S., & Casey, D. (2015). Are there relationships among racial segregation, economic isolation, and proximity to green space? *Human Ecology Review*, *21*(2), 113–132. ANU Press. https://openresearch-repository.anu.edu.au/handle/1885/224757

Williams, T. G., Logan, T. M., Zuo, C. T., Liberman, K., & Guikema, S. D. (2020). Parks and safety: A comparative study of green space access and inequity in five US cities. *Landscape and Urban Planning*, *201*, 103841.

Appendix A
Survey Questions

1. How old are you?
2. How do you identify?

    a. Male
    b. Female
    c. Non-gender conforming

3. What is your major?

    a. Liberal Arts & Sciences
    b. Business Administration
    c. Criminal Justice
    d. Dietetics and Nutrition
    e. Licensed Practical Nursing
    f. Major not declared

4. What ethnicity do you identify as?

    a. Non-Hispanic White
    b. Hispanics (of any race)
    c. Black or African American
    d. Asian
    e. Two or more races
    f. American Indian and Alaska Native
    g. Native Hawaiian and Other Pacific Islander

5. How many semesters have you attended BCC?

    a. 0
    b. 1–3
    c. 4–6
    d. 7+

6. How often do you spend time on campus?

   a. Never
   b. Not often
   c. Sometimes
   d. Pretty Often
   e. Regularly
   f. Always

7. How regularly do you spend time in outside areas on campus?

   a. Never
   b. Not often
   c. Sometimes
   d. Pretty Often
   e. Regularly
   f. Always

8. How regularly do you spend time outside near green spaces on campus?

   a. Never
   b. Not often
   c. Sometimes
   d. Pretty Often
   e. Regularly
   f. Always

9. How regularly do you spend time with friends near green spaces on campus?

   a. Never
   b. Not often
   c. Sometimes
   d. Pretty Often
   e. Regularly
   f. Always

10. How regularly do you visit green spaces like parks or gardens in general?

    a. Never
    b. Not often
    c. Sometimes
    d. Pretty Often
    e. Regularly
    f. Always

11. How comfortable do you feel at college?

    a. Not at all comfortable
    b. Not very comfortable
    c. Somewhat comfortable
    d. Pretty comfortable
    e. Very comfortable
    f. Completely comfortable

12. Do you have a place on campus that you visit regularly in your free time?

    a. No
    b. Yes

13. Where is that place?

    a. Library
    b. Cafeteria
    c. Hallway(s) outside of class
    d. Entrance "Front porch" or exit "Back porch" of campus buildings
    e. Outside benches on campus
    f. Other _____

14. How comfortable do you feel when you are in that place on campus?

    a. Not at all comfortable
    b. Not very comfortable
    c. Somewhat comfortable
    d. Pretty comfortable
    e. Very comfortable
    f. Completely comfortable

15. How often do you socialize with friends on campus?

    a. Never
    b. Not often
    c. Sometimes
    d. Pretty Often
    e. Regularly
    f. Always

16. How often do you talk with faculty on campus?

    a. Never
    b. Not often
    c. Sometimes

d. Pretty Often
   e. Regularly
   f. Always

17. How often do you spend time alone on campus?

    a. Never
    b. Not often
    c. Sometimes
    d. Pretty Often
    e. Regularly
    f. Always

18. How important is it for you to have spaces on campus that make you feel relaxed?

    a. Not at all
    b. Not very important
    c. Somewhat important
    d. Pretty important
    e. Important
    f. Very important

19. How often do you feel stressed out while you are at college?

    a. Never
    b. Not often
    c. Sometimes
    d. Pretty Often
    e. Regularly
    f. Always

20. How often do you feel stressed out while you are inside buildings on campus?

    a. Never
    b. Not often
    c. Sometimes
    d. Pretty Often
    e. Regularly
    f. Always

21. How often do you feel stressed while you are outside building on campus?

    a. Never
    b. Not often

c. Sometimes
d. Pretty Often
e. Regularly
f. Always

22. How often do you feel stressed out about college in general?

    a. Never
    b. Not often
    c. Sometimes
    d. Pretty Often
    e. Regularly
    f. Always

23. How strongly do you identify as being a scholar or a college student?

    a. Not at all
    b. Not really
    c. Somewhat
    d. Pretty much
    e. A lot
    f. Completely

24. How often do you think about course content while you are on campus?

    a. Never
    b. Not often
    c. Sometimes
    d. Pretty Often
    e. Regularly
    f. Always

25. How often do you discuss course content with other students while you are on campus?

    a. Never
    b. Not often
    c. Sometimes
    d. Pretty Often
    e. Regularly
    f. Always

26. How often do you discuss course content with faculty while you are on campus?

    a. Never
    b. Not often

- c. Sometimes
- d. Pretty Often
- e. Regularly
- f. Always

27. How often do you eat on campus?

    - a. Never
    - b. Not often
    - c. Sometimes
    - d. Pretty Often
    - e. Regularly
    - f. Always

28. When there is nice weather, how often do you eat, talk, or relax outside on campus?

    - a. Never
    - b. Not often
    - c. Sometimes
    - d. Pretty Often
    - e. Regularly
    - f. Always

29. How much do you enjoy attending college?

    - a. Not at all
    - b. Not very much
    - c. Sometimes
    - d. Pretty much
    - e. A lot
    - f. Very much

30. Overall, how happy are you?

    - a. Not at all
    - b. Not very much
    - c. Sometimes
    - d. Generally
    - e. Pretty much
    - f. Very much

Appendix B
Focus Group

1. Do you enjoy being a student?
2. Are you the first person to attend college in your family?
3. How do you feel about your campus?
4. Do you like spending time in the green areas on campus such as:
    a. The grassy spaces
    b. The areas with trees
    c. The benches around the quad
    d. The areas that are covered by grass outside the buildings
5. When you are outside, are you usually with friends or alone?
6. What are some words you would to describe how you feel inside the buildings on campus?
7. What are some words that you would to describe how you feel when you are outside of the buildings on campus?
8. When you are outdoors on campus, where do you spend time?
9. Can you show me where that is on our walking tour?
10. Can you identify some of the places where you spend time outdoors on campus and tell me what you do—for example:
    a. Sitting alone and reflecting or people watching or meditating
    b. Sitting alone and listening to music
    c. Sitting alone and eating
       Sitting and reading or reviewing coursework
    d. Sitting with friends and talking
       Sitting with friends and eating
       Standing alone and waiting for friends
       Standing with friends and talking before or after class
    e. Playing sports with friends
    f. Laying down and sunbathing
    g. Other

11. Do you have friends that you spend time with on campus?
12. Do you complete assignments, presentations, or homework with them?
13. Are you able to talk to professors or staff while you are outdoor on campus? For example: do you see them walking by and start a conversation or maybe meet with them outdoor during spring or summer time?
14. Do you play any outdoor sports on campus?
15. What kind of events do you participate in outdoor on campus?
16. When you are on campus, do you feel welcome in these green spaces?
17. When you think about a traditional college campus, what do you imagine it looks like and why?
18. Did you know that this campus belonged to NYU before CUNY?
19. Do you think that in the fifties NYU students enjoyed the same things on campus that a CUNY student enjoys today?
20. If you had to rate the most important part of your outdoor experience on campus, how would you rate these things:
    a. Being alone to reflect
    b. Being with friends to socialize
    c. Being able to do both
    d. Being able to eat outside either alone or with friends
    e. Being able to see professors outside of class
21. What's your favorite thing about this campus?

Index

academical village xiv, 15, 16
accessibility 73, 87
affordance viii, 26, 27, 57, 58
Agyeman, J. 89
American Civil War 3
American Republic 1
Appleton, J. 27, 29
Attention Restoration Theory (ART) xiv, 18, 37, 73, 82

back yard xiv, 37, 67, 68
Beach, J.M. 4, 8, 13
belonging 15, 19, 20, 24, 25, 31, 33, 36, 37, 40, 43, 46, 51, 53, 57, 58, 61, 65, 72, 77, 78, 79, 80, 82, 88
Berkeley University 19, 24, 25, 37, 40, 63, 72
Blaik, O. 10, 13
Bourdieu, P. 29, 74
Boyer, E. 21, 29
Brandt, N.J. 7, 14
Brier, S. 4, 13
Brint, S. J. 5, 6
Bronx Community College (BCC) 2, 11, 12, 13, 31, 33, 61, 66, 69, 71, 80, 84, 89
built environment 6, 10, 15, 27, 32, 54, 77, 78, 79, 80, 81, 83, 85, 87, 88

Cambridge 15, 16, 20
Cambridge University 2
Cardozier, V.R. 4, 13
Casey, D. 86, 90
Center of Community College Research (CCRC) 18, 29

Chapin, F. S 20, 21, 29
Chapman, P. 5, 16, 28, 29
Cimprich B. 27, 30
City University of New York (CUNY) 31, 41, 42, 80, 81, 84
Clark, K. 7, 13, 86
Cobban, A. B. 16, 29
Cohen, G.L. 24, 30
Colantonio, A. 87, 89
collegial encounters 20, 67
community xiv, 1, 3, 4, 5, 6, 7, 8, 9, 10, 11, 12, 16, 17, 18, 19, 22, 23, 25, 28, 29, 31, 32, 33, 42, 43, 46, 47, 48, 51, 56, 60, 61, 62, 64, 65, 69, 71, 72, 74, 75, 77, 78, 79, 81, 83, 84, 85, 86, 87, 89
compatibility 26, 66
'Cool Out, The' 7, 13
Cooper-Marcus, C. 19, 20, 24, 40, 65, 72
Cornell University 81, 87
Covid-19 xi, 83, 86
Critical Race Theory 88

Davis, S. 86
Deasy, C.M. 23, 27, 28, 29, 40, 44, 58, 70, 72, 84
Dewey, J. 6, 13
directed attention xiv, 18, 19, 26, 33, 68, 71
Dixon, T. 87, 89
Dober, R. 28, 32, 44, 61, 75, 84
Dougherty, K. 4, 9, 13

Edmondson, H. 19, 30, 39, 45
effortless attention xiv, 18, 19

Index

Egginton, W. 9, 13
Emergency Collegiate Centers (EEC) 4
extent 19, 26, 66, 89

Fabricant, M. 4, 13
Farley, D. 12, 13
fascination 18, 19, 25, 26, 51, 68, 73, 79
favorite spaces 19, 24, 50, 61, 98
Fein-Philips, K. 11, 13
four year college 2, 3, 4, 5, 6, 9, 17, 18, 41, 47, 77
front yard xv, 20, 37, 64, 85

Gibson, J. 27, 29, 57, 70
Glazer, J. 23, 29
Great Depression, The 4
green space 16, 19, 20, 31, 32, 33, 34, 35, 36, 37, 39, 42, 43, 46, 48, 49, 58, 66, 67, 68, 71, 72, 73, 74, 75, 76, 77, 78, 79, 80, 82, 84, 85, 86, 92, 98
Guikema, S. 86, 90

Hall, E.T. 39, 44, 59
Hall, M.R. 39, 44, 59
Halter, J. 88, 90
Harvard University 2, 16, 41, 85
Higher Education Act of 1972, The 8, 13
home turf xv, 20, 24, 25, 40, 58, 65, 72
Hutchison, P.A. 5, 13

Jacobs, J. 22, 30
James, W.18, 27, 30
Jefferson, T. xiv, 15, 16
Jordan, C. 41, 45

Kaestle, C.F. 3
Kaplan, R. 25, 26, 27, 30, 32, 35, 36, 44, 65, 68, 70, 73, 82
Kaplan, S. 18, 25, 26, 27, 30, 35, 36, 39, 44, 65, 68, 70, 73, 82
Karabel, J. 5, 6
Kerr, C. 10, 13, 86, 90
Kohl, R. 88, 90

Lasswell, T. E. 23, 29, 40, 44, 58, 70, 72, 84
Levine, D.O. 3, 6, 7, 13, 41, 42, 44

Liberman, K. 86, 90
Logan, T. 86, 90

McDowell, F. 4, 13
McFarland, A.L. 18, 30, 32, 35, 36, 39, 43, 44, 45
Mertins, P.E. 7, 14
Miles, LT. R. 88, 90
Morrill Land Grant Act, The xv, 1, 3
Moynihan, D. 23, 29
multiversity xv, 10, 86
Murphy, M.C. 24, 30

Naidoo, V. 19, 30
Nassau Community College (NCC) 75, 84
National Archives 9, 14
National Center for Education Statistics 9, 13
National Conference on Community Colleges 14
Nawaz, S. 19, 30, 39, 45
New Deal, The 4
New York University (NYU) 11, 12, 47, 61, 89, 98
Norberg-Schulz, C. 15, 30

oasis 10, 15, 46, 61, 71, 73, 74, 85
Olmsted, F. 16, 29, 32, 45, 62, 70, 79
Oxford 1, 15
Oxford University 15, 16, 20

Picciano, A. 41, 45
President's Commission of Higher Education (1947), The 4, 5, 6
President's Report on Higher Education (The Truman Report), The 1, 4, 5, 6
Princeton University 2
privilege 3, 23, 32, 87, 88, 89

Ratcliff, J.L. 3, 14
restorative experience xv, 19, 24, 25, 26, 33, 68, 71, 73

Saltrick, S. 17, 30
Saporito, S. 86, 90
scholarly identity 15, 19, 27, 31, 34, 36, 37, 38, 41, 43, 46, 51, 52, 53, 61, 71, 79, 80, 83

Servicemen's Readjustment Act (GI Bill), The xv, 4, 5, 10
Smith, R.K. 9, 14
sociofugal xv, 23, 59, 60
sociopetal xv, 23, 59, 60
Speake, J. 19, 30, 39, 45
stadium générale 16
stadium particulaire 16
Stanford University 8
State Dormitory Authority, The 11
State University of New York (SUNY) 76, 84
SUNY at Old Westbury University 76, 84
SUNY New Paltz 76, 84

Tenneson, C.M. 26, 30
Trow, M.A. 3, 14
Turner, P.V. 2, 14, 15, 16, 28, 29, 30
two year college 2, 3, 4, 5, 6, 7, 8, 17, 18, 41

Ulrich, R. 26, 30, 40, 45
University Heights campus 11, 12

University of Georgia 1, 14
University of North Carolina at Chapel Hill (UNC) 1, 14
University of Virginia 15

Waliczek, T.M. 18, 30, 32, 35, 36, 39, 43, 44, 45
Walton, G.M. 24, 30
wellbeing 15, 17, 18, 19, 31, 32, 33, 34, 36, 39, 40, 42, 43, 46, 51, 52, 53, 62, 63, 66, 71, 73, 77, 79, 80, 81, 82, 83
whiteness 88, 89
Williams, T. 86, 90
Wischemann, T. 19, 20, 24, 40, 65, 72

Yale University 2, 11

Zajicek, J.M. 18, 30, 32, 35, 36, 39, 43, 44, 45
Zirkel, S. 24, 30
Zook, G. 2, 4, 14
Zuo, C. 86, 90

For Product Safety Concerns and Information please contact our EU representative GPSR@taylorandfrancis.com
Taylor & Francis Verlag GmbH, Kaufingerstraße 24, 80331 München, Germany

www.ingramcontent.com/pod-product-compliance
Lightning Source LLC
Chambersburg PA
CBHW070558170426
43201CB00012B/1875